Ulrike Elsdörfe

Interreligious Encounter on *cura animarum*

Pastoral Care and Spiritual Healing

edited by

Daniël Louw
(Stellenbosch)

Ulrike Elsdörfer
(Frankfurt)

Stéphan van der Watt
(Tokushima)

Volume 2

LIT

Ulrike Elsdörfer

Interreligious Encounter
on *cura animarum*

ECPCC and ICPCC documents and reports
from 1972 – 1998

LIT

The volume is dedicated to
Werner Becher and Dietrich Stollberg.

Umschlagbild: The cover is designed by Ulrike Elsdörfer.

Thanks to DGfP (German Association for Pastoral Care
and Counselling) for various forms of support.

Gedruckt auf alterungsbeständigem Werkdruckpapier entsprechend
ANSI Z3948   DIN ISO 9706

Bibliographic information published by the Deutsche Nationalbibliothek
The Deutsche Nationalbibliothek lists this publication in the Deutsche
Nationalbibliografie; detailed bibliographic data are available in the Internet at
http://dnb.d-nb.de.

ISBN 978-3-643-90312-9

A catalogue record for this book is available from the British Library

©LIT VERLAG GmbH & Co. KG Wien,
Zweigniederlassung Zürich 2013
Klosbachstr. 107
CH-8032 Zürich
Tel. +41 (0) 44-251 75 05
Fax +41 (0) 44-251 75 06
E-Mail: zuerich@lit-verlag.ch
http://www.lit-verlag.ch

LIT VERLAG Dr. W. Hopf
Berlin 2013
Fresnostr. 2
D-48159 Münster
Tel. +49 (0) 2 51-62 03 20
Fax +49 (0) 2 51-23 19 72
E-Mail: lit@lit-verlag.de
http://www.lit-verlag.de

Distribution:
In Germany: LIT Verlag Fresnostr. 2, D-48159 Münster
Tel. +49 (0) 2 51-620 32 22, Fax +49 (0) 2 51-922 60 99, E-mail: vertrieb@lit-verlag.de

In Austria: Medienlogistik Pichler-ÖBZ, e-mail: mlo@medien-logistik.at
In Switzerland: B + M Buch- und Medienvertrieb, e-mail: order@buch-medien.ch
In the UK: Global Book Marketing, e-mail: mo@centralbooks.com
In North America: International Specialized Book Services, e-mail: orders@isbs.com

Inhalt

Preface

This publication refers to ICPCC (International Council on Pastoral Care and Counselling), and to ECPCC (European Council on Pastoral Care and Counselling); both issues are introduced in reports from various conferences and congresses, in articles and lectures. AAPSC (African Association for Pastoral Studies and Counselling) is presented by its early publications.

Three main subjects are documented by original sources:

1. Aspects of ECPCC history in its encounter of Jews and Christians unto 1998
2. Documents concerning intercultural and interfaith encounter from the beginnings of ICPCC unto 1995
3. Beginnings of the care and counselling movement in Africa unto 1995

The discussion starts with the relation between psychology and religions, as they were based in western societies. It aims at the special impacts of the *intercultural and interreligious encounter on "cura animarum": the relation between psychology, religion and indigenous worldviews.*

Since the author is German, her personal knowledge is best on the German and European scene. Being a theologian and interreligious scientist and a researcher on pastoral care and counselling, the author has combined her interest in different religions with the cultural implications of psychology used in pastoral care and counselling throughout its history among different cultures. The history of ECPCC will be presented – as far as there are documents available. This means: the first president of ICPCC, Werner Becher, has collected private documents. He made these texts available to use them for the evaluation of the beginnings. Nearly every of the early

1

conferences of ICPCC is documented by a volume of its proceedings. There are journals, especially from the 1980s and the 1990s in Great Britain, being very helpful to re-construct the issues which were discussed in the first decades of the conferences on pastoral care and counselling, mainly in Europe.

The encounter of religions in theory and practice of pastoral care and counselling will increase. It has begun with the encounter of Jews and Christians at the European Conferences in Lublin 1981 and Turku 1985, and it was followed by accesses to interreligious encounter as they were presented ten years later at the congresses in Nordwijkerhout 1991, and in Toronto 1995. The congresses in Ghana 1999, in India 2004 and in New Zealand/Aotearoa 2011 impressed with a vivid surrounding of different religious and cultural traditions; this changed the researchers' perceptions of pastoral care and counselling to a broader inclusion of the cultural aspects of the network of ICPCC.

An extended reflection on the inner development of the encounter of Christians from many different denominations with members of the Jewish religion shows the ecumenical and interreligious character of the movement as it was founded in the 1960s and 1970s in Europe. Aspects of ICPCC's interreligious and interfaith encounter are presented by lectures on different religions' accesses to PCC, mainly given at ICPCC's congresses in 1991 and 1995, when the movement turned to a global perspective.

Interrelations between modern psychology and indigenous world-views, as they are implied in the cultural encounter, will be discussed. Selected articles are presented and lectures delivered by individuals from their special religious or indigenous origin. The documents being used in this publication are typical for many others, mostly deriving from internal discussions. Two volumes published by the AAPSC in the 1990s on the state of discussion on pastoral care and counselling in Africa give insights in the cultural diversity of the movement.

Pastoral care and counselling has its basis in different theological and spiritual approaches as well as in the various methods and schools of psychology. From its beginning it aims at an encounter of different theoretical positions in psychology and theology, at an encounter of different points of view, of different traditions of religions and denominations of Christian churches, of individual lifestyles and personalities. It aims at the coexistence of different individuals and social groups, and at the reconciliation of former antagonists. This has a special impact on the *encounter of religions*. Personal encounter, dialogue, meetings and conferences are the pastoral care and counselling movement's original methods, and by this the documents show ICPCC's intention to build a reliable international, intercultural and interreligious community.

There is a large group of Christian denominations represented in ICPCC – a special impact is placed on the encounter of members of Protestant denominations and Roman Catholics, as they were predominant in the conference in Lublin 1981, in regarding the gap of "East" and "West" in Europe and in trying to overcome the history of World War II with the holocaust. The meetings of Roman Catholics and Protestants is documented in the use of locations and university units from both denominations as well as in texts written by researchers from both churches throughout the entire period of ICPCC's activities.

Some of the national assocations for pastoral care and counselling in Europe have reduced their activities, others have increased, and they now have a strong organizational culture. They already could celebrate their 40th anniversary, as it is the case in Germany. Others – in Hungary and Poland – were founded in recent years, after the 1989 political shift in Europe. All European societies are challenged to encounter religious diversity in their own traditions – that newly emerged in Europe as a consequence of migration of labourers and refugees. Islamic psychologists and caregivers work in Europe, and political units such as the European Council in Brussels and local administrations support those activities.

Societies in Africa have a long tradition of coexistence among religions and indigenous world views. Healing – one of the big impacts of indigenous traditions – is regarded as a colourful expression of different accesses in the field of "cura animarum". Whole-

3

ness represents a common goal of indigenous healing – traditions. Spirituality is the means and medium of "curing souls in Africa".

Researchers from Asia/Philippines and from South America/Brazil fill the gap to complete this study as a publication on the "global network of ICPCC".

Correspondance, reports, articles on the history of PCC in different countries and continents, lectures – altogether there exists a broad fundament of information.

Within the documents different ways of writing the term "pastoral care and counselling" occur, depending on the time and location of the writer. In order to maintain the original historic documents no efforts were made to unify the orthography.

The texts being in use mainly are "historical" – some of them are unpublished until now, some of them were published in internal journals: recent documents on intercultural and interreligious encounter in pastoral care and counselling are various, and it will exceed the possibilities of this study to imply the new developments. The collection of early documents aims at a deeper understanding of the actual discussion, and it may enlarge the awareness of interreligious aspects in ICPCC: from the history of ICPCC's intercultural and interreligious encounter to the present challenges and interrogations.

Seen from the perspective of historical succession: the first meetings of the participants of the movement for pastoral care and counselling were held in Europe – later on names changed: some of the meetings were regarded as "European conferences", others as "congresses", others belonged to the circle of "International congresses", though the places were situated in Europe.

Thanks to all those who contributed by giving articles, lectures and information.

Ulrike Elsdörfer

4

1 Caring for souls – cura animarum

Ulrike Elsdörfer

Caring for souls is an important and prominent task religions have fullfilled ever since their beginnings. In the 4th century of the Christian time spiritually inspired men and women fled the big city of Alexandria in Egypt to find some rest and time to contemplate on their Christian faith – and to have an encounter with God. In the Christian tradition these men and women were later on called: fathers and mothers of the desert.

At this time the earliest version of the later institution of monasteries, the "lifestyle" which Christian nuns and monks practice, came into being. Whatever these fathers and mothers of the desert found out in their isolated situation – sooner or later people came to ask them for advice and spiritual direction. They became well known and appreciated for their wisdom and ability to understand and spiritually guide the souls of their peers.

During centuries of Christian rulers and churches in power – in Europe and later on in the colonized and "christianized" world: people who practiced their faith in contemplation and in silence, mostly with little accesses to power and glory in the religion's outward representation, had an important impact on theological and spiritual developments in Christianity. They were regarded as the "specialists for the soul" – practitioners of "cura animarum".

Caring for the souls – Sufis practice it in Islam, Buddhist monks and Hindu Gurus do it as well; caring for the people's souls is one of the tasks a Shaman priest from an indigenous religion has to fulfill –

spending his own vivid energies to save a soul from the influence of bad spirits.

Caring for the souls: at the end of the 19th and during the entire 20th century it seemed that this evolved to become the special occupation of psychotherapists from many different origins. Predominant was the European influence of Freudian and Jungian depth psychology, which became the fundament of many types of humanistic psychologies with their special accesses to individuals and society. Religions in their impacts on the individual's soul were regarded in very different ways: many psychologists confronted religion, regarding it as destructive for modern man's psyche; others at least denied religions' implications as a positive factor for human development, others implied some aspects of religion in their systems. The critical view on religion – especially in the Jewish and Christian tradition with its suppression of emotions by an overwhelming doctrinal power – was abundant; it took time to rediscover the positive aspects and the importance of religious qualities. Some fundamental characters of religions, as they are newly discussed in anthropological sciences, gained importance again for the psychotherapeutic scene. The significance of "symbols" and "rituals" sooner or later was re-discovered by the psychological systems.

Caring for the souls – cura animarum: at the end of the 19th and in most parts of 20th century this subject seemed to become a matter of methods and medicine – far from any traditional religious impact.

In Europe as well as in America, where many of the European founders of psychotherapy lived after they had fled fascist regimes, churches had begun to lose their influence on defining morals by dogma and by guiding people. The result of this was an increasing challenge for the individual to find a structure and a meaning in life and to cope with the everyday implications of fast changing life in industrialized societies.

To enhance the development of "living human documents" of the Christian faith: this was the definition Arnold Boisen gave on combining psychology and theology; Boisen was one of the founders of the "movement of pastoral care and counselling" in the USA[1]. Finding psychological stability in a surrounding of mainly disturbing social circumstances, coping with challenges for the mind and with increasing scientification of every action – the 1920s in the USA gave a rich insight in the many changes of society and therefore provoked to have a new look at the basic needs of people in respect of *cura animarum*.

Boisen, a protestant theologian and pastor, partially in his lifetime himself was a patient at a psychiatric clinic; as a client he was confronted with the different accesses to curing psyches, as medicine provides, and he began to combine these insights with the knowledge on spirituality and the doctrines of theology, as he had learned in his study terms. In his later years he became a lecturer of practical theology and a teacher of the new idea and method of "pastoral care and counselling". He was concerned to give those "souls" voice who were neglected by fast changing societies and by the religious institutions of his time. His idea of using the knowledge of psychotherapy in a positive way for religion aimed at an inclusion of the "losing (not lost!) souls". This was not dedicated to be an act of charity towards merely helpless individuals, but it was meant to give a new and fresh impulse to criticise and renew his society and within this society the churches.

The humanistic and therapeutic view of the founders of the "pastoral care and counselling – movement" spread out in the USA, and in the second half of the 20th century institutions have developed for teaching "clinical pastoral education", a sophisticated method for psychological and theological trainings.

Howard Clinebell[2] and others brought this movement and its methods of training to an international stage, teaching and training many theologians from most parts of the world. They brought the

---

[1]   Arnold Boisen lived and worked in the first decades of the 20th century in the USA, as a pastor and as a lecturer of theology

[2]   Howard Clinebell is one of the most important researchers, teachers and practitioners of pastoral care and counselling. He founded an institute for the teaching of the method of CPE in Clarement, California, USA, in the second half of the 20th century.

implications of psychotherapy to the systems and practice of caring of souls and counselling in their most different religious traditions and various cultures.

Pastoral care and counselling then was taught and practiced in Europe, in Africa, in South and Central America, in India, Australia, New Zealand, in the Philippines, Malaysia and Japan; numerous Protestant traditions, but also Catholic and Orthodox churches opened their seminaries to the implications of depth psychology and other models of psychological theory and practice, to enrich their poimenic thoughts and teachings and their everyday practice. Many of the countries mentioned had a multi religious and multi cultural character, and within the special social climate of their societies pastoral care and counselling gave the churches options for encounters with members of other religions.

In order to exchange knowledge, experience and theory practitioners and researchers of pastoral care and counselling met in different parts of the world. Their encounter and exchange led to a clear structure of conferences and congresses all over the world. The initiating and very important first congress took place in Edinburgh/Scotland 1979, and here the ICPCC (International Council on Pastoral Care and Counselling) came into being. The ICPCC meets every fourth year, the continental meetings take place in the same rhythm, always held two years after the International Conferences.

Prior to the formation of ICPCC a rotation of meetings of Christian and Jewish counsellors and psychotherapists was instituted. First known as "European conferences", the participants of these meetings gave them a structure under the title: ECPCC (European Council on Pastoral Care and Counselling).

Part I

2 ECPCC – European Council on Pastoral Care and Counselling

Congresses

1972 *Conference on Clinical Pastoral Education in Arnoldshain, Germany*
Ev.Akademie Arnoldshain

1975 *Conference on Pastoral Care and Counselling in Rüschlikon, Zürich*
Formation for Ministry

1977 *Ökumenische Studienkonferenz für Seelsorge und Beratung in Eisenach/Germany*

1981 *European Conference on Pastoral Care and Counselling in Lublin, Poland*
Lublin Catholic University
Religious Values and Experiences in Pastoral Care and Counselling

1985 *European Conference on Pastoral Care and Counselling in Turku, Finland*
Pain and Power in Pastoral Care and Counselling

1989 *European Conference on Pastoral Care and Counselling in Assisi, Italy*
Pax et Bonum: Coping creatively with Chaos

1993 *European Conference on Care and Counselling in Debrecen, Hungary*
Pastoral Care and Counselling between Tradition and Transition

1997 *European Conference on Pastoral Care and Counselling in Ripon, Great Britain*
Riches, Rivalries and Responsibilities

2001 *European Conference on Pastoral Care and Counselling in Janské Láznj, Czech Republic*
Cura Animarum – Possibilities for the cure of souls in Europe today

2005 *European Congress on Pastoral Care and Counselling in Sigtuna, Sweden*
The Secular and the Sacred – Exploring spirituality for our time

2009 *European Congress on Pastoral Care and Counselling in Belgium, Leuven*
Prophetic Pastoral Care and Counselling

2013 *European Congress on Pastoral Care and Counselling in Göttingen, Germany*
Pastoral Care and Counselling: Borders and Boundaries

2.1 History

Ulrike Elsdörfer

Education in care and counselling nowadays is an essential part of theological education within the European Churches. This is a fact in Western Europe since about 25 years. In Eastern Europe institutions for Pastoral Care and Counselling have come up in the last decade. Here is presented a survey on the development of care and counselling in Europe from the early beginnings in a post – war Europe suffering from its division into the two blocks of "East" and "West"- unto the various challenges Europe is facing in the second decade of the 21st century.

"Formation for Ministry" was the title of one of the first meetings of European theologians in Switzerland 1975 – to discuss the outcomes of the new movement of pastoral care and counselling in Europe. "Basic goals were to share experiences in formation of ministry in the light of different cultural factors and especially to underline the differences in theoretical presuppositions. Those goals were met, but we also began to become more aware, more conscious that something deeper, broader and more profound than a professional and pastoral conference was 'forming' the 'life story' of the movement."[1] It was one of the founders of the movement of pastoral care and counselling who many years later wrote these remarks.

---

[1] Keith Parker: Rüschlikon 1975, Formation for Ministry: Memories, Dreams

Which were the "living human factors" forming individuals, lives and societies in Europe in 1975?

Student revolts had begun to spread all over Western Europe. The world beyond the "iron curtain" wasn't really taken into consideration when speaking of lively movements in Europe at that time – besides the revolts in Hungary 1956 and in Czechoslovakia 1968. Churches were busy to develop contacts between their partners in the Eastern and Western parts of Europe. Having these connections in between both parts of the divided country was important especially for the German churches. Within their membership there were family ties connecting people in Dresden and Hamburg. A movement for peace and reconciliation in Europe (Christliche Friedens-Konferenz) gave a frame for meetings of Western and Eastern theologians, sharing an idea of a human and even spiritual form of socialism deriving from certain theological roots from the Resistance – Groups in Nazi-Germany. Especially Czechs from the Prague University were dominant on the Eastern side – being familiar with the ideas that led to the revolution in Prague in spring 1968. Altogether this predominantly was a protestant movement, as the Roman Catholics at this time had their own way to deal with the gap between Western and Eastern Europe. As it will be shown later on, the Catholic University of Lublin was the only state related Catholic University in the entire Eastern European World of that time. Karol Woityla, the later Pope John Paul II, was its most prominent professor of philosophy.

The meeting in Switzerland 1975 was not quite the first. Before theologians from Holland and the United States met in Utrecht 1966, others from Great Britain and the U.S.A. had their meeting in London 1968, and then was a broadly supported meeting in an academy of the German Protestant Church in Arnoldshain/Frankfurt/Main1972. A big impact was laid on this meeting in Arnoldshain. There Heije Faber wrote: "The Europeans who were there were to a great extent pioneers, people who knew they were

---

and Reflections, in: the a.p.p.c. Journal Association for Pastoral Care and Counselling, 1985

working on something very valuable, who often, however, were isolated and working under difficult circumstances, who were looking for fellowship and cooperation, but who sometimes had to find the way to each other and learn how to cooperate, who were afraid to expose themselves and at the same time longed for understanding and inspiration."[2]

They were willing to spread out their movement to all parts of Europe, but actually it very seldom found relevant roots in Latin Europe – this being perhaps a problem of the languages, of mentalities and of the predominant denominations in special regions of Europe. Care and counselling didn't really fit so much in the structures and the basic theological systems of the Catholic Church. There always were some persons teaching and practicing psychology in the Catholic faculties in Europe, but this mainly took place in the English speaking part of Europe or in countries like Germany where the English speaking influence was important.

Going back to the beginning of the 1970s: Parker spoke of "dreams", others spoke of the "implementation of education in pastoral care and counselling", and others were convinced that this method will be an important tool in the whole renewal of Christian ministry.

International Conferences as an institution were born, an organization of ongoing publications was founded (the Newsletter of the International Committee on Pastoral Care and Counselling) – and the movement was thought to spread over all continents – and actually did within the following years.

In the 1970s in Europe "learning and training in so many different cultural and political contexts was the big unknown" as Keith Parker[3] wrote[4]. Today it is quite usual for everybody to meet and

---

2 Werner Becher: Arnoldshain 1972: Clinical Pastoral Education for Pastoral Care and Counselling, in: European Contributions to the International Conferences on Pastoral Care and Counselling from Arnoldshain to Ripon, p. 16
3 Keith Parker is one of the founders of the movement. He was professor of Practical Theology in Rüschlikon, Switzerland.
4 Keith Parker: Rüschlikon 1975, in. Werner Becher: European Contributions … , p. 22

face the problems of different cultures within Europe, one only has to cross a street in one of the bigger European towns.

Eastern Germans in the 1970s were closed up in their isolated political world beyond the "iron curtain", and again Parker wrote: "There was a sense of fear and awe around their very presence in the first two or three days until their humanity and Christian faith was expressed through parts of the program, workshops and simple contacts."[5]

Behaviour, thinking and even the social impacts of Eastern European societies made it difficult for their people to easily close up to the "americanized world". On the other hand: learning from Eastern Europe in its special traditions and "deeply rooted minds" wasn't fully appreciated in the West in those times. And psychology wasn't a predominant science in the socialist world.

Regarding this background the two conferences for care and counselling in Eisenach 1977 (then Eastern Germany) and later on in Lublin/Poland 1981 contributed to an encounter for peace and reconciliation with the European history of the 2nd World War as well as with the then current division of the world into the two political block-systems.

The conference in Lublin/Poland was outstanding, as the Catholic University was the host, as a psychologist and psychiatrist of this university was involved in the preparations for the conference. What's more – a Jewish rabbi was praying with the members of the conference when visiting one of the biggest concentration camps the Nazis had installed in Poland. Under the impression of the visit in this concentration camp some of the lectures which were given got a very special impact. Later on there will be cited some parts of a lecture of Irene Bloomfield, a psychiatrist of Jewish and German origin, then living in London. In Lublin she was teaching about stereotypes and prejudices in religious culture.

Berard Coleman, an Irish clergyman, gave an impression of this important European meeting. His diary gives insights in the whole atmosphere of those days, which he thought to be much bigger than

---

[5]   s.a., p. 23

only a conference on a scientific subject. Again it was a feeling of the "life story of the movement". "There is an anticipation of something larger than the conference right from the beginning – a sense that what is going on 'on the outside' will have an important bearing on what goes on at the conference deliberations. It is West meeting East, and at least for some of us, our first contact with the communist world."[6]

The presence of the Jewish Rabbi and his family clearly showed the issues which separated – especially in this Polish surrounding with its sad history. The Jewish Rabbi celebrated a Passover, and the conference invited the 27 Jews still living in Lublin – being the survivors out of once several thousands. Three of them attended the celebration. "One stepped forward. He was small and square but powerfully built. In a strong voice he addressed us like a prophet from the past. It was almost as if he had just come down from the mountain himself. He told us, in Polish, of his own faith in God, of his faith in the future, and he gave his benediction to the group of ministers and clergy sitting around the table. The sight of this humble worker standing in the seminary refectory and speaking forth his faith with strength and conviction was most giving ."[7]

Another impression: "The prayer pronounced by Rabbi Smith at the Crematorium where 1000 bodies were disposed each day, moved all of us … it was a prayer of forgiveness … a moment of grace."[8]

Solidarnosc, as an issue of the conference's surroundings, came up, and everybody realized that this wasn't of the sort of average trade unions all over the world. It was "more embracing"; for the Irishman it was a sort of "Sinn Fein"- experience – the movement which formed the Modern Ireland with all its difficulties.

They visited a place of Marian pilgrimage: For the Irish clergyman this place was not really comfortable, for he himself did not feel "at home" with its world. A Polish Catholic bishop was preaching, addressing the actual political needs and problems of the country.

---

[6] Berard Coleman: Lublin 1981, in: European Contributions …, p. 46

[7] s. a.

[8] s. a.

Surprisingly a Lutheran pastor found out: "It was biblical ... evangelical ... it was Christianity".[9]

The Conference was about an "ecclesia" a "gathering" – with these words and many thanks to the people running the event, Coleman finishes his diary.

It was interesting that several members of the conference in Lublin, even the president Werner Becher, were willing to give a speech at this awful place of Majdanek, the concentration camp. They all restrained from having this speech. Werner Becher later on published his then unpublished speech: "I have asked myself many times during the past days whether I as a German have anything at all to say here. Even the fact that several of my relatives, whom I never knew were murdered in concentration camps in Poland and also not far from here in Auschwitz/Oswiecin, would not be a "justification" for doing so."[10] And Zidzislaw Chlewiński, the Polish host, even did not dare to speak the words he later on wrote down: "No historian can render their most personal tragedy, their immense suffering. We believe that it has all been written down in "the book of eternal life". In this place human hatred and fear were at their peak, the prisoners often tried to help one another, there was a great deal of kindness, love and forgiveness and courage in the protest against humiliation. The most unfortunate were not those hundreds of thousands of martyrs who were put to death, but rather those who committed murder and who created the ideology of hatred and death, and manipulated other people in order to implement their plans full of hatred.

The place is sacred, for it is a place of martyrdom, sanctified by blood and suffering ... "[11]

Experiences from outside were only half of this conference. Besides that theories of pastoral care and counselling were presented, there were debates especially about the way theology and psychol-

---

[9] s. a.
[10] Werner Becher/Zdzislaw Chlewiński: Suggested Meditation for a Service at the Concentration Camp in Majdanek/Lublin on September 5, 1981, in: Werner Becher: European Contributions ... , p. 93
[11] s. a.

17

ogy come together in pastoral care and counselling. Predominant on the side of psychology were the traditions of depth psychology, this time impressively used and represented by Jewish people from German origin, now mostly living somewhere in the English speaking world. Theologians, especially in the Eastern part of Europe often relied on prophetical theological traditions. These sorts of theology mostly were very challenging. That is perhaps why those Eastern European people were marked earlier as giving an "impression of fear and awe".

Irene Bloomfield presented in her speech in Lublin several ideas, such as: "Coming to know a caring and loving God has to do with caring and loving experiences in life and with people", which nowadays are "common sense" in psychology and theology. At that time they belonged to the new found essentials of the profession.

Bloomfield explained how overwhelming and sometimes destroying stereotypes of behaviour can be, when they are imposed on persons who cannot bear them completely. She presented several examples for that: one was about a priest, who is not allowed to have a private life – everything is dominated by his congregation and "calling". Another is about a pastor having to imply the whole family in an image of "perfect Christian life", an aim they often fail at. Rabbis always have to be old, with a long beard, being "fathers", and normally they should have read a lot of books.

As she explained, the members of Bloomfield's group were not of that type, though being Rabbis by profession. "All the Rabbis in the group felt too young, none of them felt they could measure up to their own congregants' stereotype of a proper Rabbi. Even the older members of the group in their forties, who were regarded as the senior Rabbis in the country, found it a startling revelation that they were fathers."[12]

Some of the colleagues' comments said that all the ideas of Irene Bloomfield, taken separately, normally would have been considered as "friendly ideas for a more democratic lifestyle"; but in this special

---

[12] Irene Bloomfield: Religious Stereotypes, in: European Contributions ... , p. 223

context they tended to develop a scenery of very tragic and dark images coming from the background of the visit in the concentration camp. At the end of her lecture she added a story from the Nazi boycott of Jewish shops in the early years of the Third Reich. Nazi guards stood outside the shop and advised Bloomfield not to get in: "You must not go in there, it is a Jewish store." And she answered: "That is just why I'm going in since I am a Jew". The SS men looked thoroughly confused saying: "But you can't be" – for she has had red hair and freckles. Obviously this seemed to be more typical for the Germans ... [13] And there were no other means to identify a person besides these racial aspects, being an important European heritage since the 19th century.

Later on Bloomfield stated that all these very moving experiences of Lublin at that time did not really imply a chance for an encounter with the overwhelming feelings arising from the experiences of Holocaust, as they were present from different aspects. According to Bloomfield there was the first meeting openly facing these items in Turku/Finland 1985.

In Lublin a Rabbi was visiting the conferences for the first time in an official manner, celebrating the Passover. It took until the next conference in Turku, that there was a Rabbi from England invited as a main speaker, and addressing the most emotional aspects of the subject "Persecutor and Victim"[14]. Though Bloomfield stated that the main vivid interest in this conference laid on the "men-women"-relation and the emerging of feminism, she at the same time thought it to be possible to face the sentiments accompanied by persecution. "The issues of equality also came up in relation to Jewish and Christians within the pastoral care and counselling movement. Only one Jew (co-author Irene Bloomfield) was present at the early conferences. Edinburgh brought a couple of Rabbis from the United States but it was not until Lublin that a Rabbi was there in an official capacity, and not until Turku that the Jewish-Christian issue could be faced openly. Another Rabbi, Howard Cooper, brought an enor-

---

[13] s. a.

[14] Title of Howard J. Cooper's lecture, London, unpublished document

mous optimism and hope in the air. The theme of the exodus, the liberation of the Jews from slavery in Egypt was with us ...

A Jewish presence at the conferences has given them a special character. It made it necessary to confront unresolved issues, to acknowledge common roots and equally ancient jealousies as a prelude to any reconciliation of unresolved internal conflicts within collective and individual psyches."[15]

As the title of the conference in Turku was "Pain and Power", the history of the European Jews' persecution found its place. "Helplessness and omnipotence" – an issue already treated before emerged again.[16] But as the actual debate on feminism and new power relations between men and women flooded over the Western world, a vivid impact was laid on these subjects. Bloomfield stated that there were tensions between people from Eastern and Western Europe, between the West and the Third World countries, between Catholic, Protestant and Orthodox as well as between Jews and Christians. "Some of these conflicts found expression in doubts about ecumenical worship, but this was no longer a major issue at Turku which hosted the 1985 conference. The issue which seemed to arouse the greatest passions was the male/female conflict expressed in terms of who went to the sauna first and who had to wait meaning perhaps who was the power and why."[17]

Bloomfield's review on the early history of the European Conferences ends in 1989, when there was a meeting held in Assisi. First of all the author emphasized that the loveliness of the landscape, the climate and the sun as well as the widespread spirituality of this place had its special charm. For Bloomfield this atmosphere helped to re-invent and re-produce an aspect of the movement which seemed to be nearly forgotten: spirituality. Focusing on psychology, on feminism, on overcoming the wounds result-

---

[15] Irene Bloomfield: The European Conference on Pastoral Care and Counselling – Assisi 1989, in: *Contact* 1990: 2

[16] Irene Bloomfield gave a lecture on this subject, together with Alistair V. Campbell, Scotland, and Padraig Berard Coleman, Ireland – unpublished documents

[17] Bloomfield: The European Conference on Pastoral Care and Counselling

ing from European history, focusing especially on the encounter between men and women, the "healing aspects of an encounter with God" unto this time were placed in a background stage.

"Coping Creatively with Chaos" was the subject in Assisi; Bloomfield especially wanted to bring in "humour" in the psychological and theological debates, so she remarked that there was an overregulation in the structure of this conference, giving no time for experiencing "chaos" lively. For her this seemed a little bit, as if the participants wanted to prevent what they were talking about.

Art, psychology and theology came together in this conference, as the Italian history presents a lot of good art and by this a new and fresh access to psychological debates and encounters.

It was one of the rare possibilities of sharing experiences between members from Southern – and Latin – Europe and the English speaking majority of the conferences.

After 1989:

A great shift for the European Conferences resulted from the fall of the "iron curtain".

Again Bloomfield reports her impressions on the time of the "iron curtain": "The first impact of being in Poland is like travelling back in time, coming from the rush and high technology of the West. It was a strange experience to see horse drawn carts and ploughs and a few cows or sheep in the threes or fours ambling across the street. Agriculture seems to have stuck at least a century ago."[18]

"When the editor talked to me about this article he wanted me to include something about the likely consequences of the recent events in Eastern Europe for the development of pastoral care and counselling in those countries. Because the events were so unimaginable at the time of our conference and still hard to take in, it is too soon to make any predictions except that as barriers break down communications at all level should be easier. So concepts and ideas should filter through more easily,

---

[18] Irene Bloomfield: Pastoral Care and Counselling behind the Iron Curtain, in: *Contact* 1982

and training programs may start where none existed before ."[19] – this is Bloomfield's last remark, ending her report in 1989.

The opening of the "iron curtain" was welcomed all over Europe. In its consequence followed a lot of financial transactions from West to East in order to develop the economies and by that the societies in Eastern Europe. Churches in some way profited from these developments, especially in Eastern Europe.

The author's personal knowledge on the recent history of pastoral care and counselling is merely about Germany. And there is no such material on the recent history available, as it still has to be researched and written. A volume on the history of the German Association for pastoral care and counselling was published in 2012.

In Germany seminaries for the education in care and counselling have been installed – the first ones in Western Germany already in the late 1970s or in the early 1980s, mainly from churches of Protestant tradition. The author's personal knowledge is about the "Seminar für Seelsorge" in Frankfurt/Main, which in its original concept existed from 1978 until 2003. Other seminaries followed within the Protestant churches in Western Germany of that time. But there existed a Catholic seminary in Trier/Germany as well, and there was a Catholic teacher of pastoral care and counselling at Graz University/Austria, Karl-Heinz Ladenhauf, and others.

Eastern Germany followed within the 1990s with Protestant seminaries in Halle, Leipzig, and Berlin. Together with the establishment of seminaries there evolved new methods of training. Depth psychology in a broader sense never had been accepted in Eastern Germany and Eastern Europe. This was predominantly because of the communist ideology which rejected psychology and gave no space in society for its ideas. Additionally for the members of the churches it was a matter of costs not to be able to pay for psychoanalytical trainings, as many persons could afford that in the Western part of Germany and Europe.

After 1990 new theoretical impulses came from family therapy and systemic approach. The German Association for pastoral

---

[19] Irene Bloomfield: The European Conferences ... – Assisi, 1990

care and counselling, founded in 1972, already consisted of several sections, concerning the methods of training. In the beginning there was depth psychology and clinical pastoral education, later on trainings in Gestalt followed, in client-centered-therapy, in family therapy and others.

Nowadays the German Association of pastoral care and counselling (DGfP) has about 700 members. Most of them are pastors or priests, some are psychologists, or have paedagogical professions and they derive mainly from the German District Protestant Churches and from the German Catholic Church. As Germany has not a system of competitive denominations as it exists in many other countries, other protestant groups besides the dominant Protestant Church (consisting of Lutheran and Reformed traditions) are very few. But they exist within the DGfP.

The character of the German DGfP has changed very much since the beginnings – though many of its members still vividly remember the times when care and counselling was a "movement". In the 1975s Keith Parker had the dream of developing a system of education in care and counselling – and this dream came true, not only in Germany but also in the Netherlands, in Great Britain and in Scandinavian countries – mostly at the cost of not representing a "movement" any longer. CPE is an institution and a part of the churches' educational systems – aiming at the trainings of "specialized personnel" – as there are hospital chaplains, pastors and volunteers doing emergency care and counselling. It seems that the "fresh impulse from the beginning", when people on one hand wanted to meet each other and on the other hand could not overcome gaps, is gone. There is a free access for everyone to many aspects of life in Western and Eastern Europe, there are no visible borders, and the restrictions of culture or religion or even from prejudices diminish.

Perhaps the title of the European conference 2005 in Sigtuna/Sweden may give a hint on the new challenge for pastoral care and counselling in Europe: "The Secular and the Sacred". As secularization is one of the results of the diminishing "East – West" conflicts in Europe, churches have to struggle for their financial and ideological survival in the societies at all, and this has a big impact on such sensitive parts of their lives as pastoral care and counselling is concerned with.

There are a lot of positive aspects from the liberalization and opening of societies all over Europe, accompanied with an increasing wealth within the Eastern parts of Europe – compared to their history. Regarding the latest developments there are times of economic crisis in some other parts of Europe. They tend to have in consequence new nationalisms and new resentments against each other.

There are negative developments in European societies as well, and they should be seen in an emerging lack of employment, especially for young people, in drug abuse, in an uncertain economic future, as it has come to be in the Southern European countries – though they still do not belong to the preferred clientele of care and counselling, as it spread out to France, Spain, Italy or Greece only in some few cases.

The churches have lost their traditional influence. And they suffer from a lot of inner struggles. This has a big impact on the employees of the Churches. There is a fear of losing jobs. Especially in the sector of care and counselling one has to face the growing market of non-religious agencies. New and old religions from all over the world came to Europe along with immigrants – from Islam, from Buddhism and Hinduism and even from smaller religions. Besides the "cultural shock", this seems to be an economic threat to Europeans.

Nevertheless there exist possibilities of a formal encounter between Muslims and Christians in their religions, not only academically, but also in congregations. Programs for "Muslim Care and Counselling" are on their grassroots. The author is involved in one of them in Wiesbaden, a District capital in Germany.

Germany especially has to face the challenges of a new uprising of racism, as the Eastern part of Germany, according to its history beyond the "iron curtain", is not as much accustomed to foreigners as the Western part of the country. And additionally the figures for unemployment are much higher in Eastern than in Western Germany. Racism tends to spread over several countries of Northern Europe, as the Netherlands, Norway, Denmark and others.

Regarding the education in care and counselling: Some CPE – teachers offer programs including members of non-Christian religions. There is a group of persons – supervisors, counsellors, psychologians and psychiatrists all over Europe – who deal with "intercultural counselling". They especially have to take into consideration the traditions and the cultural surroundings of citizens from different origins.

One of the most active groups doing "intercultural care and counselling" in practice and theory and organizing seminaries with important intercultural issues is "SIPCC – Society for Intercultural Pastoral Care and Counselling" – founded in 1995 and led by Helmut Weiss and Klaus Temme, Düsseldorf/Germany.

SIPCC is involved in CPE – trainings including Muslims in Germany. Besides that SIPCC has good connections to Eastern European churches and Theological faculties. Together they establish trainings and seminaries for pastoral care and counselling in different countries of Eastern Europe, especially in Hungary and in Poland. In these countries associations for care and counselling exist, with increasing numbers of members, and teaching and training in the disciplines represent a part of the theological education.

Regarding the contemporary discussions on religions as they are conducted at German Universities the education in intercultural counselling has to be closely connected to the studies of comparative religious sciences. It is recommendable that the University programs and trainings in intercultural subjects should be obligatory for students of all human sciences dealing with people from different cultural backgrounds.

At the big hospital – complexes in Europe there exist units of "spiritual care" – professionals and volunteers from all religions are supposed to share the rooms for their work and their meetings, to share places for their meditations and worships. Mostly it is up to them how much they are working together in actual practical service.

Care and counselling in Europe still has a moving character. It can help to cope with the fast changing European societies – and it can help not to strain back to the ancient patterns of nationalism and separatism as it seems to be a current danger in European countries in their economic crisis. And by this it can assist churches in their ecumenical work, and it can strengthen most different people in their efforts to keep in mind the gifts of spirituality which tend to fade away at least in Western European societies.

2.2   Documents

2.2.1   A Short History of Pastoral Care and Counseling in Great Britain and Its Present Challenges

Louis Marteau[20]

Louis Marteau is of Belgian origin, but he is a British citizen. He is an ordained Catholic priest and a lecturer of pastoral psychology. He has established the first seminary on pastoral care and counselling in Great Britain as an institution managed by the Catholic Church. His report on the beginnings of an encounter of psychology and theology in British churches' seminaries gives an insight in the early times of this movement.

"It is not until the beginnings of the 1960s that we find little isolated oases making their appearance in this vast desertland. But it was not until 1965 that I really came into the field myself. For some five years prior to this I had been a member of a small group of priests and analysts, engaged in an interdisciplinary discussion group, working through the problems that existed in the field of religion and present-day analytic thought. In 1965 I found myself attending the fourth session of the Vatican Council in Rome. It was here, discussing the recommendations of the Council in respect to seminary training the His Eminence Cardinal Heenan instructed me to set up

---

[20]   The article is first published in: *The Journal of Pastoral Care*, Vol. XXVII, June 1973, p. 94-99. The article is shortened by Ulrike Elsdörfer

a working party which was to consider how best to introduce the behavioral sciences into present training now that their importance had been recognized in the Council. I returned to England, and the working party was set up. As Secretary of this working party I set out on a fact-finding mission around these shores to see just what was being done. I first made my way to Nottingham to see the Clinical Theology Association founded by Dr. Frank Lake. This had begun its life only three years before, but already had established a twelve-week residential course for those who wished to progress to a more advanced level of training, having established training seminars in over ninety centres. These consisted of a two-year syllabus of twenty-four three-hour seminars run at three weekly intervals. In a short time of space CTA had formulated its method and style of training, together with the little training handbooks, which enabled it to grow into the organization which it is today. Its resources were slim and its training team minute but its enthusiasm and driving spirit, derived from its director, were to bring it to the forefront of all such training. In these early days it had taken a very specific ideology both in its theological and dynamic interpretation of man which were moderate in more recent years without loss to its prestige. In some ways one of the remarkable facts about the CTA is the way in which it has moved from being first an innovator in the manner in which it interrelated its theology and psychology, through the period of conservatism, to the present stage of open search.

The year 1965 saw too the inception o f the Diploma in Pastoral Studies at Birmingham University. This was the child of the late Dr. R.A. Lambourne, and one of the forerunners of the work now being done in various University Departments. The course was practical and professional, as well as theoretical. Training was based somewhat on the lines of that of the professional social workers, with placements, under supervision, in the various areas of medical, psychological and social work settings. The Diploma was so organized, that it could be undertaken either as a two-year or one-year, full-time course.

The Richmond Fellowship, founded in 1958 by Miss Ellie Jansen, for the rehabilitation of the mentally and emotionally sick through hostel accommodation, had grown a total of 11 houses by 1966 when the first course of studies for theological students commenced. This course covered not only general and dynamic social psychology but included social community studies. The purpose of the course was to enable theological students to understand themselves and others more fully and to work with individuals and groups more effectively. Here some responsibility within the houses was the background of the training scheme.

At Littlemore Hospital in Oxford a course was in progress initiated by the chaplain, the Rev. Martin Rogers. This had an introductory course for student theologians spread over a period of six months, during which period a group of ten students from various colleges, and of various denominations, attended for 11 days. Their time of training covered a period of some ninety hours. This introductory course aimed at being a training in ministry itself. A great deal of the course was concerned with the art of listening. The truths and skills learned were not intended to be hospital centred, or even sick centred, but those common to the total pastoral ministry in the parochial sense. There was a second-stage course which aimed to take further the learning begun in the pre-ordination introductory course, which was undertaken in two periods of ten days.

What started out as merely a fact-finding mission turned out to be a series of encounters with people with whom I found I shared a depth of understanding and concern together with a vision of this form of ministry beyond my expectations. That each in turn reacted to this was ably demonstrated by the complete openness with which they were prepared to expose their problems, difficulties, and even early mistakes. I had only expected to make a small collection of facts. On my return I discovered that I had really created a new circle of friends. I think it would also be fair to say that at the same time my visits had not been without fruit for the organizations themselves. It was perhaps the first time that an exchange of ideas was beginning to take place. Each had questions about the other, and each seemed to be prepared to examine its own in the light of this information.

In this more general area we also had the Institute of Religion and Medicine which had brought into being in 1963 by Dr. Kenneth Soddy, aiming at bringing together clergy, doctors, and the variety of disciplines working in the field of health and healing, particularly at local levels either for theoretical discussion or practical teamwork. At the request of the British Council of Churches, the Institute also embarked on a major group of consultations into the training of clergy in this area. This series began in 1965 and in the final publication of Pastoral Care and the training of Ministers which was then passed to the B.C.C. (British Council of Churches, the author) for discussion and further implementation."[21]

The following articles written by Irene Bloomfield in the 1980s and 1990s show other aspects of the European history of pastoral care and counselling, this time seen not from the point of view of a theologian, but from a psychologist and psychotherapist.

Irene Bloomfield, the author, is born in Germany; she left Germany with her family as a young girl within the time of Nazi rule. Then she lived, studied and worked in Great Britain; her work brought her in contact with Christian psychotherapists and theologians practicing counselling. Irene Bloomfield was chair of the British association for pastoral care and counselling. She visited the European conferences, and she gave delightful surveys on their proceedings and vivid experiences.

2.2.2   The European Movement for Pastoral Care and Counselling

An Interpretive History

Irene Bloomfield[22]

In the summer of 1985 the European Movement for Pastoral Care and Counselling was ten years old, not an enormous age as organizations go but for the few who have seen it struggle, develop and

---

[21]   Extracts from the above mentioned title of Louis Marteau, in: *The Journal of Pastoral Care*, June 1973

[22]   This article was first published in: *Contact* 1990:2: *The Interdisciplinary Journal of Pastoral Studies*, Great Britain

grow from its preconception stage at Arnoldshain three years previously to its birth in 1975 in Rüschlikon there has been an undoubted and marked development and change. The issues about which the still youthful movement is concerned now are very different from the earlier ones.

The themes of the first three conferences related to the practice of care and counselling, to supervision, training and learning. Subsequently meetings tried to deal with more fundamental human values indicated by the themes of freedom, spirituality, story and symbol, pain and power. The development of the conferences resembles that of a group. Individual members change but a group culture develops and is passed on from generation to generation and from conference to conference. It is not surprising therefore that earlier conferences dealt more with externals whilst more recent ones were concerned with deeper, more unconscious and more primitive areas of human emotions and conflicts. *Biblical themes.*

This has also been reflected in Biblical themes which appeared to be less significant in the earlier conferences. The theme of Exodus was first raised in Edinburgh in connection with the liberation of women. The Exodus theme continued and predominated in Lublin where the Passover meal which celebrates the exodus of the children of Israel from Egypt played such an important part. In Turku, Genesis was the predominant theme so that Cain and Abel as well as Adam and Eve and the serpent were given a good deal of attention. The question thus arises: Where do we go from here? The answer is left to future participants and the dynamic of the movement itself.

Background

The background and roots of the International Movement for Pastoral Care and Counselling are many and varied. Prior to 1972 there were a number of personal exchanges among educators and trainers in the United States and Europe. People from several countries went to the United States to be trained in the practice and theory of pastoral counselling, and the concepts of Clinical Pastoral Educa-

tion (C.P.E.) spread to other continents. There were bilateral sponta-
neous meetings particularly between Holland and the U.S. (Utrecht
1966) and Great Britain and the U.S. (London 1968). In Holland
a strong continental European adaptation occurred with research,
practice and writing which spread to most of the continent. The
work of significant father (now grandfather) figures such as Faber,
Zijlstra, and van der Schoot became widely known and the movement became more Europeanized. Formal and informal contacts increased significantly in the 1960s. In developmental terms this could
be seen as a precourtship stage.

In Britain very little was happening in the field of training clergy
in pastoral counselling skills between the end of World War II and
early '60s. In 1962, Frank Lake founded the Clinical Theology movement and pioneered a training for clergy and other church workers
in which insights from religion and psychotherapy were brought
together. A few other training programmes started in the 1960s at
hospitals and universities but each of them was going on in isolation and was largely unaware of what else was happening in this
area until the Institute for Religion and Medicine initiated consultations at the request of the British Council of Churches. These consultations were the forerunners of the Pastoral Care and Counselling
Association in Great Britain, but it was not until 1970 that the first
formal Pastoral Care and Counselling Centres were set up, the West-
minster Pastoral Foundation by William Kyle and Dympna Centre
(Roman Catholic) by Father Louis Marteau.

In 1972 an American-trained German pastor, Werner Becher,
took the initiative of bringing together a few individuals from different countries (primarily Holland, Great Britain, the USA, Scan-
dinavia, Germany and Switzerland), known for their interest in the
Care and Counselling field; seventy delegates met at Arnoldshain,
West Germany, under the auspices of the Evangelical Lutheran
Church. This could be seen developmentally as the engagement
stage. There was no certainty about a forthcoming wedding but the
parties had met, looked each other over and had a good and worth
wile experience: but they had also quarrelled and recognized areas of conflict and disagreement, largely about different modes of

training. There were areas of polarization between the formalized and systematic C.P.E. model and the as yet rather unstructured, varied and changing models especially in England. At the Arnoldshain meeting a demonstration of a C.P.E. supervision session evoked an angry response from some participants who wanted diversity and flexibility of training; they clearly did not like the notion of a "quarter of C.P.E.", so many verbatims, so many hours of supervised work and so many hours of personal therapy. This was at the same time a true appreciation of the American trainers and supervisors who had accumulated a great deal of experience and expertise; newcomers in the field could benefit and learn from this, but there were also strong fears of American paternalism which was to be resisted at any price. For all that, there was enough to be shared and valued to plan another get-together at a conference which was to take place in Rüschlikon, Switzerland, where in fact the Union was formalized.

Birth of the European movement

In Rüschlikon the International Movement for pastoral care and counselling was born. Perhaps the Union had already taken place in Arnoldshain and the actual birth happened after the Travail of those earlier years. The tensions already present at Arnoldshain continued as growing pains. There was still serious ambivalence towards the participants from North-America, a kind of love/hate relationship towards the "big father". There was also the envy and fear of being swallowed up or being told what to do by the parent body. On the other hand there was also big appreciation and gratitude for the enthusiasm and generosity with which things were shared and for the patience shown towards the rebellious children who were of course not rebellious all the time. There was also a great eagerness to learn some of the new techniques presented and to imbibe some of the "good food" handed down by some of the original father figures. One of Howard Clinebell's introductory sessions was not only memorable but also symbolic; participants were literally feeding and being fed oranges and experiencing as never before how much easier it is for most of us to do the feeding – a good reason to take up the professional roles we have chosen.

Meanwhile the European "children" acted in a characteristically Oedipal manner by staging a ritual killing off of the father. They decided to have their own conferences and to "invite" the "parents" from across the ocean but only as observers at future meetings in Europe. At the same time a European father figure was elected as the first Chairman, Louis Marteau, a Roman Catholic priest who was born in Belgium, but lived and worked in England, one of the pioneers in his own right. Having gained their independent status, the "children" then began to fight and quarrel amongst themselves. Sibling rivalry took the form of vying for approval, attention and acknowledgement. Each one wanted to be special. Conflicts arose over a number of issues such as didactic vs. experimental learning, religion vs. psychology, theory vs. practice, formal vs. informal learning. C.P.E. was seen as a highly professional training which carried with it the risk of leading to rigidity and some loss of vitality. The English association represented the opposite pole with an ongoing controversy about the need to avoid too much professionalism for the pastoral carer; the result was that in England there were no clear standards of what constituted adequate training until the late seventies.

The conferences have highlighted how much pastoral counsellors from many countries, cultures, societies and religious denominations have in common. At the same time it made each national association – each of the siblings – anxious about its own identity and individuality.

Adolescent struggles took the form of wanting freedom from all the organizational restraints. Adolescents frequently ignore the unpleasant reality of finance, and it so was with the young European movement. It had to accept that the sponsoring bodies and national organizations needed help with finance.

Another crisis centred on the drawing up of the constitution. Was it really necessary? Would it restrict freedom and growth? How could the diverse interests be accommodated? A constitution was drawn up, and it did not put the movement into a straitjacket. In fact, most of the time people have barely been aware of its existence. The fears may be justified, however. So many promising organizations seem to throttle themselves with their own rules and regulations. The pastoral care and counselling movement has resisted up to now to become an association with membership. There are no officers except for those who plan the next conference, and there is no membership fee. But there are also disadvantages; decisions can only be taken by the committee which is planning the next conferences. Attempts at getting a newsletter off the ground have been successful and they have been dependent upon the initiative of individuals like Heije Faber from Holland und Werner Becher from West Germany. Striking a balance between too much and too little organization is not easy but the fact that the movement has survived, developed and grown is not a bad achievement.

Surprisingly perhaps we are too preoccupied with our early parents and siblings as well as with our standing in relation to allied professional disciplines such as psychoanalysis, psychotherapy and counselling to give much thought to the religious and the spiritual dimension or to be explicit about God. This did not mean that the pastoral element in pastoral care and counselling was ignored. It was perhaps taken for granted whilst professional status and recognition was something many pastoral counsellors still had to struggle for.

The question of how the religious and counselling components could be integrated, whether they complemented each other or produced conflict is still with us.

It was probably not accidental that the theme of "The Spiritual Dimension in Pastoral Care and Counselling" first cropped up in Eisenach, East Germany, the state which does not officially recognize the existence of God. It was the theme of the Lublin conference at which tensions about ways of worshipping together in an ecumenical setting became paramount.

Although written into the Constitution that we are in the "Judeo-Christian tradition", it was only in Lublin that the movement acknowledged for the first time it was a Judeo-Christian movement in that a rabbi was present in an official capacity. The common origins of Jewish and Christian traditions were celebrated by Rabbi Daniel Smith in a Passover meal, a very moving and memorable occasion for all present; the Polish nuns and students who had gone to enormous trouble to get the correct ingredients for the meal made it truly festive. The Polish priests and German pastors and the Jews and Germans sharing this Passover celebration made it a remarkable historical event itself. There was a realization that something had taken place.

The conference also tackled issues of mature and immature religion and reflected a distinctive growth in self awareness as well as the beginning of a willingness to look at ourselves, at our prejudices and at the shadow side of our lives as individuals and groups. We were brought face to face with the evil that man can do to man at Majdanek Concentration Camp. One of the Americans cried out: "And to think that those who did this were men, too!". It would have been difficult to go through the experience of what had been hell on earth and come away unchanged. It forced us also to look at the potential for evil that resides in each of us.

Prior to Lublin was the first International Congress which took place in Edinburgh and which attracted four hundred participants from the so-called first, second and third world countries; this contrasts with the approximately one hundred and twenty who attended the 1985 European Conference in Turku. The very size of the Edinburgh Congress changed the nature of the meetings. Something is gained by bringing so many people together from a vast variety of cultures, countries and continents, but something is lost in terms of closeness, getting to know people and feeling a part of the whole. Even with one hundred and twenty participants, a conference begins to have some of the characteristics of a large congress rather than a small group; in such large settings some people may not feel free to affect what is happening. The theme of the Edinburgh Congress was "The Risks of Freedom". There were some excellent papers. The congress had gone for the big names. There was still a good deal of preoccupation with gained recognition from the world at large and with gaining approval from the other authorities, from the church and professions like psychiatry and psychoanalysis. Perhaps the movement had got to the stage of wanting to identify with the "parents".

There was some irony in the extinct title "The Risks of Freedom", since it seemed that the risks of giving some freedom to ordinary participants to make themselves heard were perceived as too great. There was virtually no space for free discussion. Everything was pre-planned and organized. The organization was indeed superb, but it allowed very little freedom to the individual. This created feelings of helplessness, isolation and dependency on the leaders.

The issue of helplessness and omnipotence was prominent again at Turku as were a number of other issues from other conferences. It was obvious that there would be tensions between people from Eastern and Western Europe, between the West and Third World countries, between Catholic, Protestant and Orthodox as well as Jews and Christians. Some of these conflicts found expression in doubts about ecumenical worship but this was no longer a major issue at Turku which hosted the 1985 conference. The issue which seemed to arouse the greatest passions was the male/female conflict expressed in terms of who went to the sauna first and had to wait meaning perhaps who was the power and why.

It was at the Edinburgh congress that the meaning of the feminist movement was first raised as a major issue by the Dutch theologian Christina Halkes. She talked of it as a "freeing of men and women from the rigid structures which define both sexes in particular ways and stop them from becoming what they could be and from wholeness". Halkes described the Bible as a "fundamentally patriarchal book which restricts and restrains women, at the same time giving a message of freedom through the good news." The church and synagogue developed male dominated, hierarchical structures in which women became invisible, were silenced, had no face and no voice and no responsibility". She thought of feminist theology as "a theology of freedom and wholeness in which language and imagery of God can be expressed without sexist overtones".

At the pastoral care and counselling conferences women were not totally invisible but it was perhaps not insignificant that the first female speaker at one of the meetings was Halkes in Edinburgh. In Lublin most women were well segregated from the men and were accommodated twenty minutes away from the conference buildings. The questions which came to mind, therefore, were: Are women still perceived as too dangerous to let them get too close? Is man taking revenge on women for his dependence in early life? What perpetuates the split between the sexless virgin – mother, and the sinful, dangerous, sexual woman as represented in Mary Magdalene?

At Turku we did not shrink from the issue of men and women but it seemed that we might be in danger of simply reversing roles with women taking power for themselves and men relinquishing it. It did not happen and the hope must be expressed that it will be possible to find a more constructive way of using feminist theology, such as working together as equal partners.

The issue of equality also came up in relation to Jews and Christians within the pastoral care and counselling movement. Only one Jew (co-author Irene Bloomfield) was present at the early conferences. Edinburgh brought a couple of rabbis from the United States but it was not until Lublin that a rabbi was there in an official capacity, and not until Turku that the Jewish-Christian issue could be faced openly. Another rabbi, Howard Cooper, brought an enormous optimism and hope in the air. The theme of the exodus, the liberation of the Jews from slavery in Egypt, was with us, focussed most movingly in the Passover meal we shared together. Leslie Virgo in his accounts says this: "there are two symbols which stand out beyond all others as I look back at the experience of Poland – the symbol of the chimney of the crematorium at Majdanek, an obscene finger poking into the horizon of the camp: and a tall white candle at the Passover supper. Rabbi Daniel Smith and his wife Chani created a mysterious and powerful poetry for us all, catching us all up in a universal language, the language of the Passover".

There was at the same time a recognition that we also need our psychological insights in order to try to make sense of the experiences – of Majdanek, the pilgrimage to the shrine of the Black Madonna and the Passover service.

A Jewish presence at the conferences has given them a special character. It made it necessary to confront unresolved issues, to acknowledge common roots and equally ancient jealousies as a prelude to any reconciliation of unresolved internal conflicts within our collective and individual psyches.

The theme of conflict between Jews and Christians, Jakob and Esau, was taken up again in an excellent paper by Howard Cooper at the conference in 1985 in Turku, Finland, but the main theme of that conference was "Pain and Power" – the conflict between suffering passively adverse geographical and socio-political conditions, and fighting them actively.

2.2.3 Assisi 1989 Coping creatively with chaos

Irene Bloomfield[23]

I now come to the most recent conference. Like all previous ones it had its own particular flavour, and was very much affected by its venue. Assisi is a very special place. The beauty and simplicity of its architecture reflects very powerfully the life and work of St. Francis, and his influence was present throughout the conference.

The "Citadelle Ospitalia" is an ideal place for a conference, and all our physical needs were attended by the Italian staff with great friendliness and efficiency. Arnaldo, the conference organizer, was determined to prove that Italians can be good organisers and he made his point. There were, in addition, some special imaginative and original touches even before the conference started. Correspondence to Arnaldo was answered on a post card which was a copy of a beautiful painting by Elena Mazzari called "Dal Caos al Cosmo" which remained the symbol of the conference. Frans Andriessen from Holland, one of the pioneers of the European movement and one who always seems to have the finger on the pulse, chose pictures by Giotto as the medium of his address. He tried to help us see

---

[23] First time published 1990: 2 in *Contact: The Interdisciplinary Journal of Pastoral Studies*, Great Britain

through images what previous speakers had tried to communicate through language. For language had proved at times to be a barrier to communication; despite excellent translation something was inevitably lost. But in Giotto's picture, as interpreted by Andriessen, we were able to share in the universal and unifying language of art.

Andriessen's contribution, though the shortest – just 45 minutes – exemplified for me the essence of pastoral care and counselling conferences. He brought together insights from psychology and theology with the ease of a person naturally at home in both.

It is only now, as I am reflecting on all the conferences and what was distinctive about Assisi that I am left with the sense of the impact of colour, art and beauty in contrast to the greyness and absence of colour in some of the Eastern European countries. It would be quite wrong to give the impression that there were no beautiful monuments, paintings or icons in those countries, but they represented the preoccupations of former ages rather than being a part of the present. In Assisi it was the combination of the beauty of the landscape and art with the ever-living vision of Francis and Clare for a better, less materialistic society which had the most profound effect on me.

Francis also emphasized the enormous value and importance of our contact with the rest of the creation – the plants, animals, soil and wind. Who of us could think of "Brother Sun and Sister Moon" of Francis' Canticle without also being confronted by our current loss of respect for "Planet Earth" and its riches. It brought home the terrible tragedy of the wastefulness and destructiveness with which we deal with the earth's resources.

Such – together with many personal encounters – were my long-lasting, positive impressions of the conference. But at the same time some of its aspects were not so successful.

The theme of the conference was "Dealing with Chaos"; yet the one thing we seemed to try to avoid at any price was an *experience* of chaos; and the structure colluded with us. The time-table was tight, yet speaker after speaker went over their time cutting down on discussion and dialogue. Meals and worships had to be punctual, so the theme-centred groups were truncated, thus stopping interaction, discussion, reflection and the possibility of conflict and disagreement. I wondered if we allowed this to happen day after day because there was an underlying fear that real interaction might result in a chaos that we would not be able to deal with creatively. Some of the talks took the opposite view. Marie Josephe Glardon from Switzerland in her key note address "Chaos and Creativity" spoke of water as "the womb of all possibilities for existence and for original or primordial chaos". Immersion, she said, is a return to death, new birth and recreation. "Primordial chaos must be periodically revitalized by rituals, orgies, festivals, debauchery and creative violations." Marie Josephe's paper was a treasure trove of the myths, rituals and symbols of creation, but perhaps the possibility of involvement in primordial chaos evoked too much anxiety of what might happen if we began to experience it even in a mild form.

Frans Andriessen also spoke of the importance of chaos. "In the Bible the chaos before creation is the source of all possibilities. Chaos therefore remains with us after creation and can be the source of a new world. Coping with chaos means keeping contact with it, not declaring it merely an enemy, but seeing it also as an abyss out of which life comes forth."

The richness contained in these few passages alone could have been enough to reflect on for several sessions. It seemed a great loss that there was virtually no time to do so.

The problem was aggravated for me because of the constellation of my small group. Three of the seven members did not approve of this sort of unstructured group, did not like it and could not see the purpose of it. They had very little or no experience of such groups and were very erratic in their attendance. Only two or three members saw this group experience as potentially the most valuable forum for exploration of issues in depth, for experiencing and observing interactions and for gaining greater self-awareness.

I know that other participants had very different and often good experiences in their small groups, but mine highlighted a more general problem, which raised fundamental questions for the future. Arnaldo had been remarkably successful in attracting a substantial number of delegates from France and Spain, countries hitherto almost unrepresented at these conferences. The Italian contingent naturally was much larger than previously, and there was also a number of people from Eastern European countries which before had only been minimally presented. But in all these "newer" delegations the concept of pastoral care and counselling as it has involved in the West is virtually unknown. In consequence experience and levels of sophistication varied enormously, and for some the attempt to integrate psychological and theological insights was viewed with some suspicion. On the other hand some participants felt deprived of gaining insight into counselling because of the emphasis on the pastoral and theological. The question of how these different levels and interest can be reconciled will need some attention in the future.

That the emphasis in Assisi was very much on the religious, spiritual and theological was partly a reaction against previous conferences which had focused much more on the counselling dimension. This was particularly so in the earlier conferences in which recognition, respectability and professionalism played a dominant role, as they then did in the respective national organizations. But it was also because in Assisi religion was all around us and the influence of Francis and Clare so positively pervasive. Nevertheless this reflects another polarization or split which we have not yet managed to heal. We probably achieved the best balance between these components in Lublin where the external situation greatly facilitated the work towards inner integration.

When the editor talked to me about this article he wanted me to include something about the likely consequences of the recent events in Eastern Europe for the development of pastoral care and counselling in those countries. Because the events were so unimaginable at the time of our conference and still hard to take in, it is too soon to make any predictions except that as barriers break down communications at all levels should be easier. So concepts and ideas should filter through more easily, and training programs may start where none existed before.

It may sound grandiose and a little fanciful, but I wonder

whether our choice of conference theme for Assisi – "Dealing creatively with chaos" reflected some contact with the collective psyche of Europe which is in a state of chaos and appears to be trying to deal with it in a remarkably creative and hitherto almost unprecedented way. Perhaps there has also been a recognition at some deeper level that unless nations begin to *collaborate* to save our planet from destruction we will be doomed.

The message from Assisi that bears on this seems to be that in working collaboratively to deal with chaos we cannot shy away from conflict or try to smooth over tensions. Differences need to be identified and valued, for only then can we begin to heal the splits which still exist between us and within each of us.

3 Jewish – Christian encounter in psychology and religion

Howard Cooper is the first Jewish speaker to give a lecture on pastoral care and counselling at one of the European Conferences (Turku 1985). He is a rabbi, then living in London; his and his colleague's Gilah Dror's method aims at combining insights from depth psychology with the Jewish religion's traditional texts and rabbinic theology.

3.1 Documents

3.1.1 Persecutor and victim

Howard Cooper[1]

I would like to begin an approach to our theme with a story from my childhood. I was 6, maybe 7 years old when it happened. My background is that I was born and brought up in Manchester in a middle-class Jewish home. Almost all of the Jewish children in my road were sent to private schools some distance from their homes, but I was sent around the corner from my house to the local school. I was the only Jewish child there, in what was a predominantly working-class area. I always felt different. I was the only child who did not go to the Christian assembly each morning, but sat in the library reading. I was overweight, shy and socially ill-at-ease, while

[1] Howard Cooper: A lecture delivered in Turku 1985 – unpublished paper; the text is shortened by Ulrike Elsdörfer.

43

most of the other boys seemed thin and tough and went around in gangs. Because I could read when I went to school, I was put in a class of children a year older than me, so each year I was always the youngest in the class. Not surprisingly then, I grew up in those pre-adolescent years as an outsider, and I was teased for being fat, for being serious, for sucking my thumb in class, for not being good at football, for having long trousers when the other boys wore shorts, for being different. But whether I was picked upon or protected, it was because I was experienced (and experienced myself) as being not the same as the others. But the one area where I have no memories of being constantly ridiculed by the children was my religion. I do not remember a single anti-semitic comment, no taunts or "rich Jew" or "Christ-killer", or, as my mother remembers from her schooldays, cries of "You killed our Lord" at Easter-time.

Yet I have this one memory from when I was 6 or 7 years old. I was sitting around a table at school with some other children, drawing. Suddenly one of the boys shouted out: "Look, I can see Jesus floating on the ceiling!" I looked and of course could not see anything. But soon all the children were joining in: "Yes, I can see him, too! Can't you see him – he's up there, floating on the ceiling!" This little Jewish boy had no idea what they were talking about. I desperately wanted to see Jesus floating on the ceiling, too, but I had no real idea of what I was expected to see. All I could visualise was one of the old English coins which used to have a picture of the head of King George (the Fifth). This I did manage to see floating in the air – a bronze penny with the bald head of a dead King. "Can you see him, Howard?" the other children cried. Half-heartedly I joined in. Yes, I could see him, too.

To this day I do not know if those children were teasing me or not, if I was their victim or not. Much of my ambivalent relationship to the non-Jewish world is contained in that story. The wanting to belong, to fit in and be the same as the others – or at least not to be persecuted for being different. Yet knowing that the Jew was, and is, different – does not share that same vision but conjures up his own alternative insights to set side by side with the majority voices and view; then often pretending, as the child Howard did, that he isn't

44

really different, that he shares the common vision. And through it all, not knowing, not understanding, the motives of the non-Jew: a deep suspicion.

Were those children (and now of course I am using them to symbolize something much larger), were they reaching out to embrace me, to include me into their world, to genuinely share with me something precious? Or were they taunting me with their insiders' collusive secret knowledge, knowing that I could never "see" Jesus as they "saw" Jesus? Knowing that it is just this irreducible mystery which has forever divided the Jew from the Christian? Yet whether the non-Jewish world wishes me to assimilate into them and abandon my different status, or whether it wishes to highlight my exclusion, my separateness, my alien "Otherness" – whatever the wish may be (and paradoxically it can be both at the same time) – I want to recognize with you the impossibility of us ever understanding or fulfilling our separate destinies except in relation to each other. The fact that Jesus was born and lived and died as a Jew means we are indissolubly bound to each other – Jews and Christians – for all time. In love and in hate, with each other as the persecutor and the victim, we wrestle with each other for a blessing, as the Biblical Jacob wrestled with his mysterious night-visitor.

I want to turn from that confused child, caught up in his own way in an ancient drama, to an adult experience I had not so long ago. I was driving in London and noticed a middle-aged woman standing by the roadside talking to herself and carrying a battered suitcase and shopping-bags containing all her worldly possessions. They are not an unusual sight now in our inner cities, these rootless, homeless, sometimes mentally ill men and women, young and old, the dispossessed and disadvantaged of our country, ignored or condemned by the Government.

The traffic I was in was moving slowly. This woman peered into my car as it approached. "You fucking Jew" she shouted. Nobody had ever said that to me before and I was shocked. That was my first instantaneous reaction – shock. But my next immediate reaction surprised me even more: with all my being I wanted to drive my car into that woman, to destroy her in my anger and my pain and my confusion. Of course I did not; and of course on reflection I began to understand that my desire to harm her was my way of dealing with my own deep hurt which she had touched, a hurt which did not originate in that one knife-wound she had stuck into my psyche, nor in my personal childhood experiences of being the Jewish outsider. No, the origin of that hurt is part of my collective experience: that angry woman, splitting out her words like a curse, echoed for me every anti-Semite who, without cause or reflection, cursed or condemned, abused or tortured or murdered the Jew through the ages.

That poor woman, the victim of the social and cultural and spiritual deprivation of the late 20th century turned in her fury and her despair on the Jew. And for a moment she, that poor deprived woman, became my persecutor, and I was her victim. At that moment history was abolished and we could have been in any country in Christian Europe over the last thousand years.

Now I could at this point try to tackle head-on the underlying questions raised by these remarks.

What is it about the non-Jewish world – and in particular, historically, the Christian world – that needs the Jew to be the victim of its loathing and its murderous impulses?

And what is it about the Jew which attracts persecution? Is there something in the Jewish unconscious which fatally attracts such anger and hatred, such fear, such awe?

Yet something in me draws back from facing theses questions directly. It may be the enormity of the subject, of the fact that these questions have been asked many times before, or maybe it is the pain involved in opening up these ancient wounds which still bleed inside me. Whatever it is, I would like to take a different route for the moment and deal with some of these questions elliptically, as it were, merely hinting, suggesting, reflecting some thoughts and feelings on persecutor and victim. I want to do this looking with you at a story from our common tradition about the first persecutor, Cain, and the first victim of murder, Abel. My hope is that by drawing you into the mythical world of the Bible story, the feelings raised by these themes can be contained and held, as they can be contained and held and worked upon in that other mythic world we have created for ourselves: the sacred "hour" of psychoanalysis or psychotherapy or counselling.

Let me explain this a little. By describing the story of Cain and Abel as a "myth" (and the counselling sessions as "mythic"), I am not using the word in its debased sense – the product of 19th century rationalism – where it has come to mean that which is opposed to "reality". On the contrary, I want to convey that myth is "the most important form of collective thinking", providing us with a model for illustrating and understanding all human actions and interactions. It is not opposed to reality but a true revelation of reality. A myth contains and allows the deepest human feelings; so too does the therapeutic encounter between counsellor and client. Also there is an exemplary honesty in the narrated myth, or the therapist; in both cases there is the break with profane time and integration into primordial time and space represented by the session, and in the Biblical narrative.

If we look together at Cain and Abel we may be able to catch the glimpse of our own persecutor and our own victim – those parts of ourselves that we carry into all our encounters, whether it be between us here in this conference, or in our own families, or in our roles of counsellor or client, or in our identities as Christian and Jew. Let us look at ourselves, with the text as a mirror.

Our Genesis text is terse, enigmatic, gloomy, disquieting. It begins:

"And Adam knew Eve his wife and she conceived and gave birth to Cain; and she said: I have acquired a man for God" (4:1).

Her words are in fact ambiguous. They could also be translated: "I have formed a man with God 's help" or even "I have formed a man, just like God has done". We do not know what her words mean. But we should be alerted, and disturbed, by this first ever birth. Whether the words are said in humble acceptance, or joy, or as a cry of triumph over Adam at her own creative powers which are like God's – and they have received all these interpretations by Jewish interpreters in the past – their effect is to deny Adam his role as the father, the co-creator of Cain. She speaks, but Adam is not acknowledged. He is excluded. In the previous chapter, in Eden, Eve has been told she will be emotionally dependent upon her husband – "your desire shall be to your husband and he shall rule over you" (3:16). Now she gives birth and she speaks. She does not speak to Adam. She just speaks into empty space.

Eve never speaks to Adam in any of the Biblical scenes. Adam never speaks directly to Eve. There are several monologues, but no dialogue. The first human couple, Adam and Eve, never speak to each other. They both speak a great deal, but each one for themselves; two solitary individuals at the beginning of time, locked inside themselves, victims of a great silence between them.

We know for ourselves the different silence we inhabit – the full, rich silence where nothing needs to be said between two people, because all has just been revealed, or is about to be revealed; then there is the silence of indifference, and absence of relationship; and there is the angry silence when much should be said, a persecuting silence, denying and attacking the other. How much there is silence, in that absence of words! How fraught with significance that first silence seems to be: it is into that silence that Cain is born.

Normally in Biblical stories the child is named by one of the parents, often the mother. For example, later on in this chapter (4:25), after the story of Cain and Abel has been completed, we are told: "And Adam knew his wife again and she gave birth to a son and she called his name Seth/Shayt".

This is the accepted narrative and psychological form: the woman gives birth to a child and that child is then named. But we see in our original text (verse 1) how Cain arrives in our text fully-formed as it were. It does not say there that Eve gave birth to a son, whom she then calls Cain. No: "She gave birth to Cain". He is denied a childhood. And her words confirm this: "I have acquired *a man*". She does not see a child, only the man he is to become. The Hebrew word used here for "man" is "Ish", which has a root meaning of strength, courage, and support. Cain is already the victim of his mother's needs: "I have acquired a support" she says. The child who grows up knowing that his mother needs supporting and pro-

48

tecting – and only he can do it – what does he do with his assertiveness and his anger and his hatred which also needs to be expressed *against* mother? We know that often these emotions are repressed only to lie in wait in the unconscious ready to explode.

Let us move to verse 2:

"And again she gave birth, to his brother Abel; and Abel was a keeper of sheep, and Cain was a worker of the ground".

With so much invested by Eve in her first-born Cain, what emotional energy has she for the younger brother? This time after the birth there are no words. Again we see no child and no naming on the child. Only a name: "Abel", "Hevel", which in Hebrew means – "nothing, emptiness, a breath, transience, vanity … " His name expresses both his relationship to his mother – and his destiny. Abel never speaks in the text; he is empty of words. He is the silent victim; speechless he faces death, unable to cry out to his brother or to his God.

We want him to cry out before the blow is struck – "Stop! What have I done to deserve this? Why me?" But the voice of the victim is not heard. So what irony when God says to Cain:

"The *voice* of your brother's blood cries out to me from the ground"(v. 10). It is only *after* his death that we hear that Abel has a voice.

But we are jumping too far ahead. We are still in verse two, with the scene being set. Cain – his name means one who forms or shapes fashions material – he works the ground. Abel keeps the sheep. Separate occupations. What can we say about this?

We have seen that Cain seems to be Eve's special possession, the favourite son. We would not be surprised then to find that the father has angry feelings towards this first born. Do we see any signs of this in our story? Not directly, but in the previous chapter in genesis we have been told that the fruit of the ground has been cursed by God (3:17); and what does Adam do – he teaches Cain the inferior occupation – Cain will work the ground! So not only is Cain the victim of his mother's needs – he is also the victim of his father's jealousy. The younger child, Abel, becomes father's favourite. Any mother may develop some strongly negative feelings toward her second child in these circumstances. He becomes Abel – nothing, emptiness. Now of course we are creating here an imaginary picture of this first family's life. The text shows no family life. But this did not stop the rabbis of old weaving stories around these characters. These stories and legends were called Midrash. Which means "exploration/searching", and sometimes these imaginative word-pictures they created hit upon an essential truth. There is one Midrash which tells how Eve dreamt that Cain was eagerly drinking the blood of Abel. He will not stop, whatever Abel says. She tells the dream to Adam who separates the two boys, fearing that this is a portent of Abel's death. He teaches each a different occupation, but nevertheless Cain still kills Abel. In other words, Eve's death-wish toward her younger son turns into a self-fulfilling prophecy.

So the first two verses give us in their own allusive way the dynamics of the family life of this first, mythical family. We have silence, favouritism, jealousy, and then the absence of the parents: Adam and Eve, who are named in the beginning of the story, then disappear – first father (mentioned only in the first verse), then mother (who disappears after the second verse). Cain and Abel have only themselves – they will live out all the tensions in the family. The first and almost fatal "generation gap" in history, and most inevitable.

Let us take the next few verses together:

After some time Cain brought of the fruit of the ground an offering to the Lord.

And Abel also brought, he himself, from the firstborn of his flock and of their best parts; and then the Lord had regard for Abel and his offering.

But for Cain and his offering He had no regard; and Cain was very angry, and his face fell.

Well, if we have talked about the favouritism of Adam and Eve we must now talk about the favouritism of God. Why does God choose to discriminate between the two brothers? How is one to understand God's arbitrary way of handling them/us, playing one man against the other, turning them into irreconcilable enemies? Is God trying to make the point that injustice is inherent in the human condition?

Traditional Jewish commentators have gone some way in responding to these questions. They point out that although Cain is the first to bring his offering and Abel seems to be copying him, we should nevertheless note carefully the way which the story is told. Whereas Cain brought "of the fruit of the ground", in general, Abel brings something more personal: "of his flock". And the text emphasises it is "the best part". And the way the Hebrew is constructed give the curious impression that "he brought *himself*", in other words, again something more personal is offered as well as the material sacrifice. This double suffering, of the person and the sheep is echoed then in God's response which spells out that "the Lord had regard for Abel (the person) *and* his offering (the sheep)", again distinguishing between the two. So the style of the text seems to suggest that God's favouritism has to do with the different consciousness of the two brothers, with Abel wanting to give more of *himself* to God. Does this then satisfy us as an explanation for God's behaviour? Is it that injustice is built into the fabric of our world and all brothers are not equal, or is there another meaning behind God's actions?

But let us delay judgment for a while. Once the brothers do experience that one is chosen and the other is not, once Cain becomes the victim of God's choice, what happens? Naturally he becomes very angry. He has tried to please and he has been rejected. These offerings are his idea but they or he is not good enough. Again, he is not good enough. Through no fault of his own, not good enough for father; through no apparent fault of his own, not good enough for God. Used by his mother, abused by father, and rejected by God in favour of his nothing-brother. And he becomes very angry. At first he does not seem to have any way of expressing this anger. Except that "his face falls". Something happens to his appearance, his manner. He has been "facing up" his situation in life until now, but this is more than he can endure.

So God speaks to him, faithfully mirroring Cain's two reactions to his rejection:

"And the Lord said to Cain: Why are you angry? And why has your face fallen?" (v. 6)

But having acknowledged Cain's feelings in such a straight-forward way, God's remarks form a sentence which is classified by Jewish tradition as one of the five verses in the Bible whose sense is *impossible* to unravel. As I understand it, the sentence should be translated like this: "If you do well, will you not be lifted up? But if you do not well, sin is crouching at the door: its desire is for you, but you can/must master it" (v. 7).

Cain is disappointed, humiliated, resentful, angry – we too recognize these emotions. But the text suggests that we have the possibility of facing up to our frustrations and going beyond them. Let me paraphrase and explain the verse: "If things go well for you, do you not feel uplifted? But if things do not go well for you, "sin" lies in wait for you ready to overwhelm you but you have the possibility of overcoming these negative emotions."

"Sin" here are all those chaotic emotions and energies inside us that threaten our quest for wholeness, all those destructive inner forces which prevent us living to our true potential, all those unconscious urges and feelings which block or stunt our growth as human beings.

When Cain's repressed anger does come onto the surface, verses 6 and 7 give us a key moment in the development of human consciousness. The deepest passions that we have do not have to be denied; they wait to attack like an animal crouching at the door, but you can master them, channel them, transform them, make poetry out of them. (There is an unconscious pun in the Hebrew – the verb used here meaning "to master" also has a secondary and complete different meaning of "to speak in parables, to make proverbs or poetry").

For a wonderful moment the text then opens as an alternative to that angry silence between the brothers. Just as the parents never speak to each other, so the children are never shown speaking with each other. But something in God's enigmatic words creates the opportunity for Cain to initiate the first dialogue in human history. Perhaps it is the recognition of Cain's anger and pain and resentments – and the momentary vision which is offered of a way of working on them – which enable Cain to speak to his brother for the first time. Verse 8 begins:

"And Cain said to Abel, his brother … "

And we wait. Mouths open, we wait for the first words to be spoken between human beings. Trembling we wait in anticipation of dialogue, of communication, of words that will move between brother and brother. The Hebrew word "ach" means brother not only in the biological sense: in the Bible it is the symbol of peer relationship between all human beings. So, for the first time Cain, representing all mankind, will speak to his brother, will speak to us all, will speak *for* us all. We wait and we have been waiting ever since. Because there is a gap in the fabric of the text. The verse continues not with the expected, the longed-for, word, but with action: " … and it came to pass that when they were in the field, Cain rose up against Abel his brother and killed him." In the absence of dialogue, death enters the world for the first time. The antithesis of dialogue is – murder. We face here the power of words, and the pain that results from the absence of words.

Cain, the victim of his mother's needs, the victim of his father's jealousy, the victim of God's revelation that we have a degree of freedom to transform our destructive passions; Cain the victim is overwhelmed by his inability to speak to his brother and in desperation invents a way out. The escape from the inability to speak *now* takes the form of the one action which will make any speech in the future impossible-murder. Victim becomes persecutor in order to escape from the need to speak, to find ways to speak, to break the silence. But the destruction or death of the one who is persecuted does not solve the problem. The persecutor remains the victim of his own conscious or unconscious inability to enter into dialogue; he remains the victim of his own inability to transform destructive feelings into creative achievements. The persecutor remains the victim of his own unconsciousness. Attempting to solve the problem "out there" it remains alive and poisonous "in here". And both persecutor and victim loose out.

Cain's sudden hunger for dialogue is frustrated. We know from the work of Melanie Klein that when a "baby is hungry and his (or her) desires are not gratified … hatred and aggressive feelings are aroused and (the baby) becomes dominated by the impulse to destroy the very person who is the object of all his desires". Cain destroys what mother and father have created (or in Eve's words what mother and God have created). The attack on Abel is also an attack on mother (where the first frustrations are encountered), on father, and on God (where the recent frustrations are encountered). But it is Abel who suffers, the first scapegoat, the first innocent victim of projected anger.

Or is he entirely innocent? What has Abel done, or not done, that should make him into the victim? We must look at the *victim's* psyche as well as the *persecutor's*. What do we know of Abel, the victim? We have his silence of course – withdrawn into himself, he makes no moves to initiate dialogue either. And when Cain does summon up the courage to speak, to break the silence, where is Abel, his brother? He *is* present, he is there, he *is* the one who will die. But does he not see Cain's need, Cain's desperation to reach out across that great wall of non-communication? Cain *is* unable to speak, but Abel is unable to help him to speak. There is a great failure of imagination here on Abel's part. He is unable, maybe unwilling, to take responsibility for being open and receptive to his brother. Surely Cain's inability to speak at the crucial moment must be connected to Abel's inability to be open to receive what Cain wished to say. How well-named he was!: Abel/Hevel – "nothing, a breath, transience". Abel, making himself into nothing, insubstantial, ephemeral, contracting in upon himself, evading Cain's hesitant approach. Abel/Hevel "vanity"; that empty pride in his own detached, self-preserving distance.

At least Cain acknowledges that he has a brother! Seven times (verses 2,8 twice, 9 twice, 10,11) the text brings to our attention this fateful word – brother. But every time it is Abel who is the passive object – Abel is always Cain's brother. Cain is never Abel's brother. This is vanity indeed – the illusion that Abel can exist continually denying his common humanity with his brother, Cain.

And alongside the denial of relatedness, and alongside the aggressive silence surrounding Abel, we see that he is not content to bring an offering *the same* as Cain's; his offering has to be better, and he has to put all of himself into it. What is he trying to prove? Is it a need for the praise and approval from God which he did not get from his denying mother or silent father? Does he need evidence that he is indeed loveable? What insecurities are lurking here that make him need to be special, better than Cain? What fears of his own worthlessness make him offer only of the best he has? And what feelings are raised in Cain by his brother's striving for perfection?

You can see that we have some powerfully persecuting unconscious attitudes in Abel's denial of relatedness, in his silence, in his pursuit of holiness at the expense of his brother. Do all victims consciously or unconsciously attract their fate?

Is there no such a thing as an *innocent* victim?

Again, we approach the heart of the matter. A part of me wants to say: "No, there is no such thing as an innocent victim." But another part of me cries out against this – we could all speak of victims in the past and in the present who have been unjustly accused or persecuted or condemned to a life of misery and degradation; or who have died a death unjust by all standards, human or divine. Sometimes the arena is the family, and the abuse is physical or mental violence, or sexual cruelty. Sometimes the area is political, and the abuse is brainwashing, or torture, or murder, or the deprivation of fundamental human rights or dignity. My fear is that when we use the victim's unconscious against them – "oh, something in the victim attracted their fate", are we just not adding our own voice to that of the persecutor's?

So where can we go from here? We have moved from some initial remarks about my own experience, to some reflections on Cain and Abel as persecutor and victim and persecutor. Do the complex dynamics of that first family throw any light on our interaction as

Jews and Christians? My hope is that by looking at this one specific kind of intense relationship where persecutor and victim roles so easily arise, it may help us see the way in which the polarization operates in other contexts, too, for example between East and West, black and white, men and women.

Wherever such apparent "opposites" emerge, wherever such splitting takes place – "You are bad and I am good" – something in us is being denied. We know that the longer we remain unaware of what it is in us we are forced to live out. And the persecutor/victim dynamic is one of our most universal expressions of unconsciousness.

In an analysis of antisemitism – and particularly in an analysis of the psyche of both partners, Christians *and Jews* – we have a case history in collective psychotherapy with implications which reach far beyond antisemitism itself and the fate of the Jews.

Jews often claim that antisemitism has appeared over the last 2000 years wherever and whenever they have settled into a host community. In fact this is not true. Jewish settlements have for long existed in India and China without attracting any particular attention, and the Jews of Spain from the 9th to the 13th century experienced a golden age of harmonious co-operation and interaction with their Muslim brothers. Nevertheless we know that anti-Jewish feeling does have a long and bloody history. Various views have been put forward as to what is in the Jew that attracts persecution: there are Jewish traditions which lead to separateness and exclusiveness – dietary laws and marriage laws for example have traditionally made it difficult for the Jew to mix freely in the non-Jewish world. I suggested that Abel's distancing himself from his brother generated anger in Cain. Essentially Jewish tradition sees chosenness as a mystery born out of God's love for this small, rebellious people. In reality there are no special privileges, only extra obligations and responsibilities.

The experience of separateness and the concept of chosenness would attract anger or jealousy, but I do not feel that this gets to the dark heart of the matter. Outbreaks of violence or repression could of course be born out of these angers and jealousies, but surely there is something more behind the centuries of pogroms and massacres and finally in our own enlightened century, genocid. When Jews are imagined as the collective embodiment of evil, with extermination as the only solution, we are dealing with a level of fantasy deep in the unconscious. This kind of irrational antisemitism can exist when Jews are in sizeable and recognizable communities or where there are only a few scattered individuals; it embraces Jews who may be rich or poor, assimilated or holding onto traditions. Remarkably the most expressive expressions of antisemitism "can be found among people who have never set eyes on a Jew and in countries where there have been no Jews for centuries."....

When God asks Cain after the murder: "Where is Abel your brother?" Cain replies in those famous words: "I do not *know*. Am I my brother's keeper?"(4:9). To that, my commentary would be that to the extent to which we do not *know* what is inside of us, to just that extent do we then deny that we have responsibility for our brother. When we do not know, do not want to know, ourselves, how can we know our brothers, our common humanity with other human beings? Lack of self-knowledge leads inevitably, tragically, to a negation of brotherhood and the denial of our essential humanity – Christians and Jews, or Jews and Arabs, or the United States and the Soviet Union, or me and the poor old woman in the street.

When the second Vatican Council in 1965 debated Jewish collective guilt for the death of Christ we were beginning to see a serious coming-to-terms by the Church of the consequences of their teachings, a coming-to-terms with the "shadow"-side of Christianity. It is only in our generation that the Jewish people living at the time of Jesus, and all the Jews of today, have been exonerated from the charge of the deocide. For nearly 2000 years all Jews were seen as the persecutors of Christ. Jesus had been the victim of the Jewish failure to recognize him as the Messiah. What happened of course was that then the roles were reversed. As Jung said: "It is the persecuted one who persecutes". The Jewish people became for Christianity the recipients of all their unconscious anger and cruelty, superstition and barbarity. Brought up in a diet of humility and meekness and compassion, what do you do with your aggression, your greed, your sexuality, your murderous rage against parental figures? From medieval times to the present day the Jew has become in fantasy the embodiment of these denied passions. Greed? You have the Jewish international financial network, collecting everything for itself, sicking dry the rest of the world. Aggression? Jews strive for world domination/Zionist expansions. Sexuality? Jews are over-sexed, lusting after Christian women. A Spanish law code of 1265 proscribes the death-penalty for any Jew who had sexual intercourse with a Christian woman – "for Christian women are spiritually the wife of our Lord Jesus Christ". And this same combination of sexuality and religious imagery I found recently in a remarkable pre-war Nazi cartoon. This showed an evil-looking old Jewish man behind which was a naked young blond Aryan woman tied to a cross. The caption said "Otto Mayer used to crucify his victim. Her bound her, naked, to a specially prepared wooden cross and raped her as soon as the blood began to flow from her wounds". Out of what unconscious was that born? And I remember my encounter with that woman in London street in 1985 – "You *fucking* Jew", she said.

I do not want here to catalogue or trace the centuries of Christian antagonist to the Jew which merged into the neo-barbarism of the 20th century's "Final Solution" to the problem. All I would say is that the experience of the Holocaust in our time argues against the pretensions of Western civilization as a whole. The phenomenon of mass murder in Europe between 1940 and 1945 means the Christian and humanistic traditions upon which European Civilization rests can no longer preserve their conviction of cultural superiority, or their belief in the inevitability of progress under their benign guidance. However, "oppression is the cultural possession of the oppressors". Christianity must look for its own shadow. As a Jew my responsibility is to look for my own blind spots. Where is my unawareness? What is there in the Jewish psyche which becomes the hook that can carry the projections? I hope that my analysis of Abel opened some possible ways of exploring this, for me, most difficult of all questions; and I hope that we can pursue these questions together later in dialogue. We do need each other now.

But I have a few suggestions on this theme – the lack of consciousness in the victim. Psychological work with victims often points to a certain innocence or naivety in them which seems to attract aggression; sometimes there is an optimism or hopefulness which seems not just a defense against their own pain but a genuine inability to believe ill of others or accept the dark side of life – of man or of God; such holy innocence in the face of the absurdity of human existence does seem to attract negative attention.

I want to point to two interconnected strands of this in the Jewish psyche: the first is a certain naivety about evil; the second is the insistence on unattainable ideals. Let me illustrate the first – the naivety about the existence of evil. Nineteen hundred years ago a great calamity struck the Jewish people. The temple in Jerusalem, the centre of religious life for the people, was destroyed by the Romans after 4 years of war. The city was occupied, the people conquered and humiliated, thousands died. The religious and social structure of the Jewish people all but disappeared. The land and the people were desolate. The destruction of the temple in the year 70 of the current era struck at the very heart of Jewish identity and Jewish survival. A small group of scholars managed to escape to a town on the Mediterranean, Javneh, and were actually given permission by the Romans to set up a school there. These rabbis laid the foundation in the decades that followed for a new kind of Judaism not built around the Temple, and sacrifices and priests. This was a revolution in Judaism – but this is not the point. Those rabbis asked themselves the question: "Why was the Temple destroyed?" Their discussions were written down and handed on through the generations. Eventually all the discussions of all the generations were written down and were put together in one massive work – the Talmud. That is how we know *now* what the survivors said *then* about the disaster that had happened to them. They said: "We know that throughout the time the Temple stood, the Torah (i.e. the 5 books of Moses) was observed, good works were practiced and the commandments were respected. Why then was the temple destroyed? "And the answer they gave? "Because our people hated each other without cause".

The leader of this school, Rabbi Yochanan, had his own opinion: "because the judges judged by the strict letter of the law – but did not go behind the letter to the truth". Rabbi Chanina had another opinion: "because no one rebuked his neighbour when they did something wrong". Other voices then gave other reasons for the destruction of the Temple by the Romans: "because there were no trustworthy people with in", and finally: "because a man was put to shame in public and no one prevented it".

Now I do not know what you make of these explanations. What I find remarkable is the total acceptance that the destruction was deserved, that the Jewish people had brought it upon themselves. "Something we have done has brought this disaster upon us!" There is no discussion of the Romans and their evil intentions for the domination and submission of the Jewish people. No, there is just the guilt – it was all our fault. You could say this shows an amazing ability to look at one's own shadow, at one's own lack of wholeness as a people and as individuals. No anger, no desire for revenge or retribution, no blaming the Romans; the victims looked inwards, and accepted the blame. This is what I meant by an innocence or naivety about evil: accepting the suffering is just, the punishment is deserved. It was not the Romans who were bad – it was us who were not good enough. Something is being avoided here …

And even after the War there have been some very fundamentalist Jewish teachers who have tried to argue that the Holocaust was the fault of the German Jews who had assimilated into German society and abandoned their own traditions.

But more representative of Jewish thinking about the Nazi persecution is a prayer which was to have been recited by Rabbi Dr. Leo Baeck in his synagogue in Berlin on the eve of the Day of Atonement in 1935. Leo Baeck was the acknowledged leader of German Jewry from 1933 to his imprisonment in the concentration camp on Theresienstadt in 1944. His temporary arrest in 1935 was in order to prevent him reciting this prayer. In it we hear the end of the victim's irrational self-hatred and guilt, the end of the naivety about evil, the end of the avoidance of reality, the end of the fear of saying: *You* are to blame as well as us.

In this hour all Israel stands before God, the judge and the forgiver. In His presence let us all examine our ways, our deeds, and what we have failed to do.

Where we transgressed, let us openly confess: "We have sinned!" and, determined to return to God, let us pray: "Forgive us".

We stand before God.

With the same fervor with which we confess our sins, the sins of the individual and the sins of the community, do we, in indignation and abhorrence, express our contempt for the lies concerning us and the defamation of our religion and its testimonies.

We have trust in our faith and in our future.

Who made known to the world the mystery of the Eternal, the One God?

Who imparted to the world respect for man, created in the image of God?

Who spoke of the commandment of righteousness, of social justice?

In all this were seen manifest the spirit of the prophets, the divine revelation to the Jewish people. It grew out of Judaism and is still growing. By these facts we repel the insults flung at us.

We stand before our God. On him we rely. From Him issues the truth and the glory of our history, our fortitude amidst all change of fortune, our endurance in distress.

Our history is a history of nobility of soul, of human dignity. It is history we have to recourse to when attack and grievous wrong are directed against us, when affliction and calamity befall us.

God has led our fathers from generation to generation. He will guide us and our children through these days.

In a sense this new consciousness of external evil was too late. The die was already cast. But in his prayer we do at last hear the anger. But what we also hear is the other strand in the Jewish psyche that I mentioned before which I believe has attracted such negative attention – the insistence on unattainable ideals.

We hear in this, the victim's deepest and most unconscious persecuting act of defiance – the insistance on a moral life, on justice, equality, human dignity and, above all, the insistence on one God. It was Hitler who was reported as saying "conscience is a Jewish invention". The uniqueness and strangeness of the Biblical idea of *one* God is still hard for us to grasp …

The scandal and the shame of our theme "Persecutor and Victim" stretches us from Cain's murder of Abel to the gates of the crematoria and beyond. And within. Again and again we return to ourselves, to Abel's silence and Cain's "I do not know". By now it is too late not to know. By now it is too late to argue that "they" are the ones who are wrong, "they" have to be fought against and opposed. By now it is too late not to know whatever is wrong in the world is ourselves, too. In the face of the absurdity and cruelty of our times there are few voices with the courage to help us look inside ourselves and offer some hope. For some C.G. Jung has provided some guidance. Talking of our individual responsibility to withdraw projections, he says of the person brave enough to work on themselves in this way: "if he only learns to deal with his own shadow, then he has done something real for the world. He has succeeded in removing an infinitesimal part at least of the unsolved gigantic social problems of our day."

For others, guidance has been provided by those victims who have been through our contemporary recreation of Hell and have survived. And not only survived but have been able to offer teaching Torah, out of their experiences. One of these, Eugene Heimler, born in Hungary in 1922 and now professor of Human Social Functioning at a Canadian University, was a prisoner in several camps, including Auschwitz and Buchenwald. I would like to end with some word of his, which I hope brings together some of the themes I have been trying to explore with you:

"It was in Buchenwald that I learned from Jews, Christians, Moslems and pagans, from Englishmen, Serbs, Romanians, Albanians, Poles and Italians that I was only one more suffering insignificant man; that the tongue my mother taught me, and my Hungarian memories and the traditions of my nation, were nothing but artificial barriers between myself and others. For essentially, as Mankind, we are one. A slap in the face hurts an Englishman as much as it does a German, a Hungarian or a Negro. The pain is the same; only our attitude to the pain differs according to the cultural pattern of the country and individual. Our dreams, each dreamt in a different language, spell out the same dream in the language of Mankind: all of us want peace, security, a life free from fear. And each in his own way, irrespective of differences of nationality or race, we seek for the meaning – or meaningless – of life and death, believe in God or deny him, cry for a woman on whose bosom we may rest our tormented head.

I learnt that within me, as in others, the murderer and the humanitarian exist side by side; the weak child with the voracious male. That I am not in any way superior, that I am not different from others, that I am but a link in the great chain, was among the greatest discoveries of my life. From then on I resolved to support those who fell, even as I had been supported. When someone was desirable, greedy and selfish, I remembered all the occasions when I, too, had been despicable, greedy and selfish. Buchenwald taught me to be tolerant of myself, and by that means tolerant of others. It may be that I would have learnt this without the lesson of Buchenwald. But I would have learnt it much later – perhaps too late".

3.1.2 Riches, Rivalries and Responsibilities in the Pastoral Counseling Setting

Gilah Dror[2]

Gilah Dror is a rabbi then working at the Eshel Averham Synagogue in Beer-Sheva, Israel. She is specialized on Jewish theology on care and counselling and already has participated at the European Conference in Hungary 1993. She is a member of the Board of The Seminary of Judaic Studies and President of The Rabbinical Assembly for Israel.

"As I thought about the subject which we are exploring today, I remembered my first encounter with Michal.

Michal sat before me – thin, round shouldered, grey-haired – but most of all with a sense of purpose about her. She had been to psychiatrists,

---

[2]   Gilah Dror: A lecture delivered in Ripon (Great Britain), 1997 – unpublished paper

doctors, counselors – and here she was. What was I to do with her – or for her? As she unfolded her story before me I learned that Michal was unable to sleep at night. She was constantly troubled. The situation had been going on for nearly six years and someone suggested to her that she should talk to the Rabbi. As Michal spoke I found myself wondering what God expected me to contribute to this moment. Even as she spoke I found myself praying and remembering what one of my teachers had said to me. "Remember that they will come to you as a Rabbi – not just as a counselor."

To my mind, pastoral counseling is taking part in the redemptive process.

In his book "Who is Man", Abraham Joshua Heschel (scholar and philosopher, 1907-1972) attempts to put into words his sense of the redemptive process in relation to human history. Heschel writes:

" ... even though God's creation retains precedence over man's corruption, man has the power to convert blessing into curse, to use being for undoing, to turn the elixir of God's word to deadly poison. His power of corruption may again and again, temporarily, for long stretches of history, destroy what God designs. However, man's wilfulness is not the ultimate force in history. We are involved in a drama dependent upon the polarity of creation and corruption. Just as creation goes on all the time, redemption goes on all the time. At the end, we believe, God's care defeats man's defiance.

God and the world are not opposite poles. There is darkness in the world, but there is also this call: "Let there be light!". Nor are body and soul at loggerheads. We are not told to decide between "either-or", either God or the world, either this world or the world to come. We are told to accept "either" and "or", God and the world.

It is upon us to strive for a share in the world to come, as well as to let God have a share in this world."

Much of what Heschel says about the redemptive process in history is true with regards to the redemptive process in the "history" of the individual as well, and the counseling process at its best is a part of that redemptive process.

The story is told about a Hassidic master who once declared that previous to his birth, an angel showed him a tablet divided into two columns. On the right side he read: "In order to know the Torah, a person must have no compassion on his family. If one works to satisfy one's family's needs, there will be no time to study the Torah". On the left side he read: "One, who pities people, is pitied in Heaven. One must care for one's family even beyond one's strength, for our families' lives are dependent upon us." As he read on in the tablet, he saw that invariably the right side of the tablet presented a polarity in relation to the left side – yet each side presented a teaching of the Torah. He told his disciples that while he was engrossed in the thought of how difficult it is to find a way of behaviour which would reconcile these antinomies, he suddenly heard the words: "Mazal Tov, a child is born." He finished his story by saying that he remained wondering, and since then has continued to search for the way to follow both rules, however contradictory.[3]

Recognizing the polarities, the dilemmas inherent in life, and working toward their successful "management" is honoured in Jewish tradition. Moreover, there is a "counseling" tradition in Judaism, and rabbis have long been seen as "counselors", although there are different styles of rabbinic counseling, based on a variety of personal and theological approaches."[4]

Why would a person living in an era of increasing secularization come to a rabbi for counseling?

Cynics might say that one comes to a rabbi for counseling because it is often cheaper than other counseling services. Certainly this is true in some cases, however, many people feel that it is "safer"to speak to a pastoral counselor than to someone else. Even

---

[3]   Louis I.Newman, The Hasidic Anthology, Schocken Books, New York, 1963, p. 54

[4]   See for example Neal Rose: "Toward a Rabbinic Counselor Model: Based on a Humaistic Approach to Hasidic Stories:" Journal of Psychology and Judaism, Vol. 13,1, Spring 1989, p. 19; Norman Saul Goldman, "Midrash and Interpretation: Toward a Model of Rabbinic Counseling", Journal of Psychology and Humanism, Vol. 13(1), Spring 1989, p. 37; Jack H. Bloom: "Psychotherapy and Judaism today", CCAR Journal: A Reform Jewish Quarterly, Summer/Fall 1995, p. 59, and I.David Oler, "Operational Theology and Psychotherapy: a new perspective in Pastoral Counseling", Proceedings of the Rabbinical Assembly, 1995, p. 145

more important is the sense that both the counselor and the counseled are engaged not only in the process of listening to one another, but also in the ongoing challenge of trying to hear God's voice. Sometimes, it is specifically the desire or opportunity to discuss personal issues in relation to religious traditions, practices and norms which brings one to a pastoral counselor, familiar with these aspects of life.

What the rabbi uniquely brings to the counseling situation is a spiritual approach based on the wealth of Jewish tradition – texts and scriptures, history and thought – through which the search for the voice of God has traditionally taken place throughout the history of the Jewish people – a tradition which has always been aware of the ongoing struggle of the human condition – a tradition which has retained a vision of a joint partnership between humankind and God in the process of *tikun*, the ongoing process of perfecting one's self as well as the world. The Rabbi traditionally is sensitive to the nexus where Israel, God and Torah meet. In this context, Israel represents the community, as well as the individual – the human dimension. Torah represents the sacred texts through which God's word has been revealed to us. Torah is meant to engage the human mind and heart. Torah is meant to encompass our entire life and being, and yet, it is oftentimes elusive. Israel and Torah by themselves are not enough, because even Torah can become idolatry if we lose sight of the fact that it is a mere pointer to something beyond our human grasp.

In this paper I would like to reflect on pastoral counseling by thinking through the relationship between two triangles. One triangle, that of the counselor, congregant and Creator, represents all who play a part in the pastoral counseling situation. The second triangle represents the complex interplay of riches, rivalries and responsibilities to which the first triangle must relate if it is to offer an effective response to the problems of the individual in search of redemption.

The inter-relation of these two triangles creates in my mind an image of the Star of David – two intersection triangles – each informing and illuminating the other.

Creator

riches rivalries

counselor congregant

responsibilities

Riches, rivalries and responsibilities permeate many levels of our being. They, at once, work upon us, cause to be conflicted and tested, and yet, they contain the seeds of a special integration of character, spirit, and mind which may potentially uplift us and transport us from where we are to a higher level of being.

Midrash[5] tells us: "Three gifts were created in the world. If a person has obtained any one of them, he has acquired the desire of the entire world: if he has obtained wisdom, he has obtained everything; if he has obtained strength, he has obtained everything; if he has obtained riches, he has obtained everything. But when? When these things are the gifts of God, and come to him through the power of the Torah, but the strength and the riches of flesh and blood are worth nothing at all, and they come not from God, they will be taken from him at the end."[6]

Solomon Schechter (theologian and scholar, 1847-1915) summarized rabbinic theology in relation to the question of poverty and riches by saying:

"The kingdom of God is inconsistent with a state of social misery, engendered through poverty and want. Not that Judaism looked upon poverty, as some author has suggested, as a moral vice. Nothing can be a greater mistake. The Rabbis themselves mostly recruited from the artisan and labouring classes, and some of we know that they lived in the greatest want. Still, they did not hide from themselves the terrible fact that abject poverty has its great demoralizing dangers. It is one of the three things wich make man transgress the law of his Maker.

But even if poverty would have this effect, it would be excluded

---

[5]   A genre of rabbinic literature consisting of exegesis and homilies based on biblical texts

[6]   Numbers Rabbah, Mattot, xxii,7

from the kingdom of heaven, as involving pain and suffering. Judaism was preserved from the mistake of crying inward peace, when actually there was no peace; of speaking of inward liberty, when in truth this spiritual but spurious liberty only served as a means for persuading man to renounce his liberty altogether."[7]

Schechter adds: "The Rabbis were not satisfied with feeding the poor. Not only did they make the authorities of every community responsible for the poor, and would even stigmatize them as murderers if their negligence should lead to starvation and death; but their great ideal was not to allow man to be poor, not to allow him to come down in the depths of poverty. They say: "Try to prevent it by teaching him a trade, or by occupying him in your house as a servant, or make him work with you as your partner." Try all methods before you permit him to become an object of charity, which must degrade him, tender as our dealings with him may be."[8]

Thus, poverty is not an ideal. True, there are some Jewish sources which regard poverty in a positive light. One such source declares: "God examined all the good qualities in the world, but found no quality so good for Israel as poverty, for through poverty they fear the Lord. For if they have no bread to eat, no raiment to wear, no oil for anointing, then they seek the Lord of mercy, and they find Him."[9]

However, material riches are also not an ideal in and of themselves. They are to be used thoughtfully to help establish the kingdom of God in this world. Not always are we aware of the dangers of riches. Ideally, material riches should be intermeshed with spiritual riches which have the power to imbue them with meaning and purpose.

Rivalries abound in human societies. A Jewish kabbalistic prayer says: "God, make it so that if I triumph over my friends, that I may not gloat in my victory over them, and if I lose, that I may not seek excuses to explain how it came to be that my friends out

---

[7]   Apects of Rabbinic Theology, Schocken Books, New York, 1961, pp. 110-111
[8]   See above, p. 112
[9]   Tanhuma d.b., Eliyahu, P.181

did me."[10] Some rivalries are obvious and some are less so. Some are productive and some are counterproductive.

It happens sometimes that a balanced sense of responsibility may turn rivalry into spiritual riches. The Talmud tells us (Bava Batra 21A) that when scholars vie, wisdom mounts. The presumption underlying this statement is that the scholars' rivalry is for the sake of Heaven and that each scholar motivates the other to sharpen arguments and better organize thoughts. In fact, clashes of views, which might otherwise develop into divisive rivalries, may become the basis of pluralism founded on mutual respect.

Sometimes it seems that responsibilities are the very backbone of Jewish living.

Midrash tells us that God admonished human beings in the following manner: "See my creation, how wondrous and beautiful, and all that I have created was created for you. Think upon this, and do not corrupt and desolate My World, for if you corrupt or desolate it, there is no one to set it right after you."[11] We are given 613 commandments in order to help us fulfil our responsibilities to God and to each other. Nevertheless, there are often conflicts and struggles related to the responsibilities which we face in our day to day lives.

The biblical story of Abraham, Sarah, Hagar and their children sheds a unique light on the problematic involved in dealing with our responsibilities, in the light of our riches and our rivalries. It also points in interesting directions with regard to pastoral counseling.

The story in Genesis Chapter 16 is familiar to us all. Abraham and Sarah are childless. Sarah suggests to Abraham to take Hagar, her maidservant as a concubine in order that they might have a child. The domestic situation becomes difficult. As soon as Hagar conceived, her mistress becomes lowered in her esteem. Sarah deals harshly with Hagar and the situation goes from bad to worse. Sarah comes to Abraham and says: "My wrath be upon you! … The Lord judge between me and you¡'Chapter 21 picks up the story with the

---

[10] Avraham Amos, Derech Kalah LaKabbalah; pe'er HaKodesh-Moyal, 1996, p.76

[11] Midrash Rabbah Kohelet, Vii, 28

birth of Isaac, son of Sarah and Abraham. Sarah demands on Abraham: "Cast out this slavewoman and her son; for the son of this slave shall not share in the inheritance with my son, Isaac." Abraham is distressed. But the text tells us: "But God said to Abraham: 'Do not be distressed over the boy or your slavewoman. In all that Sarah says to you: *Shema BeKola*. Harken to her voice.' And Abraham sends Hagar and Ishmael, their son, away.

In the context of this story, the Hebrew words "Shema BeKola" – "Harken to her voice" – are not the equivalent of the English "Do as she says", or "Follow her instructions". The Hebrew words "Shema LeKola" could mean "Do as she says" or "Follow her instructions", but, here "Shema BeKola" means delve into the inner voices beneath the surface of that which is being said to you. "Shema BeKola" means: "listen carefully to all that she is expressing." Perhaps the key to a greater understanding is in listening to the*tone* of voice which may convey some of what she is trying to communicate. Perhaps the key of understanding *"all* that Sarah says to you" is *"BeKola"* – literally: *in the sound* of her words and sentences – not in the actual words, suggestions, or instructions – which she offers you. Listening to the voice and to the tone implies trying to listen to the very soul of the person who is speaking – and not only to the spoken words.

Why did Abraham not pick up on this distinction between "Shema BeKola" and "Shema LeKola"?

The text tells us that Abraham was distressed in regard to Ishmael and Hagar. We also know that Sarah turned to Abraham in anger and in frustration in search of a solution to the problem. Perhaps Abraham's personal involvement in this domestic situation made it particularly difficult for him to think clearly. Nevertheless, despite his personal involvement, Abraham plays the role of the pastoral counselor in this story.

The story tells us that Sarah came to Abraham repeatedly with her frustration and anger. We know that Abraham tries to be attuned to God's voice in searching for the proper reaction to the situation. God wants Abraham to hear all the inner voices with which she was struggling and says to Abraham "Shema BeKola". Abraham misinterprets God's voice thinking God wants him to send Hagar and Ishmael away.

But what are these inner voices which God wants Abraham to hear? One voice was the pain of the *rivalry*. Another voice was the responsibility Sarah feels toward the promised child and toward God. After all, *she* was admonished for laughing when the angels announced that Isaac would be conceived (Genesis 18: 12-15). As a result of this admonishment, Sarah undoubtedly knew that God was a serious factor in this whole situation. Beyond the voices of the rivalry and the responsibilities which Sarah felt, there was the voice of the *riches* which she wanted to ensure for her child. This voice which was closest to the surface, came out explicitly in the words which Sarah said to Abraham: " ... for the son of this slave shall not share in the inheritance with my son, Isaac."

Were these riches, which Sarah wanted for her son, material or spiritual riches? Couldn't they be shared in some way? Perhaps these were some of the questions which Abraham should have been asking himself as the situation developed.

In our caregiving, we need to be constantly aware of the impact which other people's riches (material and spiritual), or lack thereof, may have on our own perception of them and on our choice of how to function in relation to them. No less important is an awareness of our *own* riches, or lack thereof, which may colour the choice we make in relation to our caregiving. Was Abraham and Sarah's higher social and economic status in relation to Hagar a factor in Abraham's understanding of the situation?

Why did Abraham not pick up these questions? Why did he understand God's response to be affirming Sarah's demand to turn away Hagar and her son? Why did he not hear that God was telling him was to listen carefully and with sensitivity to all that Sarah was saying to him but not necessarily to adopt her suggested solution?

The Bible tells us that Abraham also laughed when he heard that he and Sarah would have a child (Genesis 17:17), but Abraham was not admonished for laughing. God merely responded to Abraham's laughter by reiterating his promise to Abraham. Perhaps the fact that he was not admonished is an indication that despite Abraham's unique relationship with God, Abraham's spiritual growth was still incomplete. Perhaps this too made it harder for him to realize the full import of the various voices involved in the story. Had Abraham been able to hear more of God's voice, and had he been able to hear more of the inner voices embedded in Sarah's demand, perhaps he would then have been able to better hear Hagar and Ishmael as well. Perhaps he would have found a way to uncover the blessing which was meant for each of his children.

As readers of the biblical story, we know that there were *two* blessings – one for Sarah's son Isaac, and one for Hagar's son Ishmael.

This story, replete with the interplay of riches, rivalries and responsibilities, and ancient as it is, mirrors the complexity of modern day pastoral counseling and highlights several areas of particular interest in this field.

Abraham's distress and subsequent failure to help bring about a positive resolution of the problem, points to the need to maintain a calm and neutral presence in the counseling situation.

His failure to hear the nuances of God's voice serves as a reminder that one must always search for further spiritual development and insight. As counselors, our own religious experience colours our ability to integrate God into the counseling. Being part of the redemptive process implies trying to let God into the situation. This means looking beyond the social "givens" which seem at times to predetermine our solutions. Not always is the solution "either/or" – sometimes it is "either and or". Sometimes it is more complex than we would like it to be, or more complex than our initial perception would have us believe. Letting God in means looking at ourselves and at others in the "light" of God – looking for the holy light which can illuminate both the people and the situation. It means understanding that we don't always see the light immediately, but continuing to search, continuing to be open to more and deeper perceptions. Letting God in means keeping in mind, whenever possible, the search for the win/win solution – the search for the "double blessing"- elusive as it may seem at times.

The combination of religion and counseling provides the pastoral counselor the opportunity to recommend prayer, to teach prayer and to use prayer as a tool for spiritual growth and as a means of connecting to others both through study of prayer and through prayer itself. The study of prayer offers the opportunity to discuss the import of words and phrases and to observe their impact on our lives.

The combination of religion and counseling also offers the opportunity to argue with God and to thank God. It has the potential to help us find inner strength through connection with God, and to find peace through involvement with community. Just by being there, the pastoral counselor is able at times to convey God's blessing, understanding, and support to a person's struggle.

Finally, we are given the opportunity to emulate God's ways, to be compassionate, understanding and purifying as we serve our communities.

Michal came to me complaining of restlessness and inability to sleep. In the course of our conversation she mentioned to me that this problem started at the same time that her father died. Since then she had not prayed, nor had she talked much about her feelings in regard to her father. In teaching her the basic prayer for mourners and suggesting that she "complete" the mourning process by personally reciting this prayer on a regular basis during the next few months, we were able to close one circle and open a new one. Somehow, during that time, restful sleep came to her at long last. During our few meetings Michal told me of her relationship with her siblings and of her feelings towards them in relation to their differing understandings of their responsibility toward their aging parents. She also spoke to me about her feelings in relation to her late father's inheritance. Riches, rivalries and responsibilities were in fact the issues with which she was dealing. But pastoral counseling enabled her to open up new spiritual avenues through which she was able to find peace.

In the traditional "MiShe Berach" prayer for the sick, we pray for "Refuat HaNefesh u'Refuat HaGuf" – healing of the spirit and of the body. In pastoral counseling we attempt to touch people's minds, and souls, in the hopes of participating in and promoting the process of healing of mind and body. This is done through the search for relevance and meaning, in which we apply our experience in studying not only counseling techniques, but also in studying rabbinic sources and hermeneutics based on critical analysis of texts and stories, to a search for deeper meanings in the stories brought to us in the counseling setting.

Rivalries are not only present in our congregants' lives, but in ours as well. A pastoral counselor might be tempted to compete with other counselors in order to establish a personal reputation in the field of counseling. At times the professional rivalry stems from the rivalry of competing belief systems. People might come to a pastoral counselor asking for an amulet or a charm designed to "fix" the situation. Sometimes what is wanted is an incantation or an exorcism. If one is unwilling or unable to provide this service, other counselors are prepared to do so. The struggle is to determine the limits of one's ability to provide counseling, with integrity in regard to one's own belief system, and taking into account that there are competing belief systems at work which may be held both by the person requesting the assistance and/or by other counselors. It is necessary to set one's limits in a responsible way with an awareness of one's own limitations, acknowledging that a certain degree of flexibility is possible and even desirable in order to accommodate other points of view.

The challenge of pastoral care and counseling is to accept our responsibilities with humility, knowing our limitations, knowing that we are not God ... yet searching at all times for the divine spark within each of us.

The Sages of Yavneh used to say:

"I am God's creature and my fellow is God's creature. My work is in the town and his work is in the field. I rise early for my work and he rises early for his work. Just as he does not presume to do my work, so I do not presume to do his work. And lest you say: "I do much, and he does little", we learn: "One may do much or one may do little; as long as one directs one's heart to heaven." (Barachot 17a).

3.1.3   Helplessness and Omnipotence of the Counsellor

Irene Bloomfield[12]

Three authors of different religious origin (Jewish, Roman Catholic and Protestant) give lectures on the same subject of "Helplessness and Omnipotence of the Counsellor" – they deal with the ambivalences of feeling helpless and at the same time assuming to have an omnipotent helper or solution. This may appear in religious based counselling as well as in clinical psychotherapy – a common issue arising in both disciplines and in the two religions.

When we are small and helpless, the world can seem a very menacing place full of dangers from within and without. So much happens in both worlds that is completely outside our control. There are some things though that seem to bring relief and comfort. Yelling is one such tactic. It can make the little boy or girl quite powerful. Just think of the little creature in its high chair howling and yelling at the top of his voice. It would take a very strong minded or very indifferent parent who could ignore such urgent calls for attention. So it seems like a very successful bit of magic for a time, but then relief does not always come instantaneously. Mother may have her hands full or be attending to something or someone else, and then his fury is terrible to behold. He is left with feelings of uncontrollable rage or outrage, and looks as if he would like to destroy the whole world, and when the rage subsides he is inconsolable, felling despairing and utterly helpless.

Another way of dealing with very frightening, or disturbing experiences and feelings is through phantasy. Selma H. Fraiberg in her delightful book: "The magic Years" describes how her little niece Jannie succeeds in taming the wild beasts of her imagination. "Jannie adopted as one of her imaginary companions "Laughing Tiger". He was the direct descendant of the savage and ferocious beasts which disturb the sleep of small children. He sprang into existence at a time when Jannie was very much afraid of animals who could bite and might even eat up little girls. When you are small and help-

---

12   written 1985, presented at the European Conference in Turku, Finland, 1985

less there are not too many solutions handy, but one place where you can meet a ferocious beast on your own terms and leave victorious is the imagination. You can choose whether to maim, banish slay or reform the brute. Jannie chose reform. All the dangerous attributes of tiger underwent transformation in Laughing Tiger. Teeth? This tiger does not bare his teeth or snarl. He laughs. Scare children? He is one who is scared. Wild and uncontrolled. One word from his stern mistress and this hulk shrinks into a corner.

Taming this most savage of beasts is paralleled by the transformation of those qualities in the little girl. The reformation of the imaginary tiger has given Jannie some control over a danger which earlier had left her helpless and frightened. Another child might stalk the tiger and shoot him with his home made Tommy gun or out-roar him or become the tiger.

These are very important experiences for the developing personality. Hard, though they may be, they help us to separate from mother and to master the fears which go with such a separation. The separation itself is both good and bad, good because it is a stage in our growth and development into separate beings. It is bad because we have to give up the sense of one-ness with mother which produce such feelings of ecstasy.

It goes on like this throughout our lives. Every gain and step forward also involves a giving up of something we had before. Other contributors will deal with some of the negative aspects of the helplessness and omnipotence of the counsellor. It is a very important, but often rather neglected subject. It is comfortable. I would, nevertheless, like to put it to you that even helplessness and omnipotence can have their positive side.

I had an experience of this process with one of my very first child patient Susie. I knew very little about therapy at that time which was just as well in this case, because it meant that I had to learn from her. She was 5 years old and since entering school had stopped speaking. She just would not utter a word, and none could make her. Parents and teachers were in despair, and brought her to the clinic as a last resort.

When Susie came to see me she went straight over to the sandbox and started busying herself, looking round at me from time to time but hoping that I would not notice. I addressed a few remarks to her back, but without any result whatsoever. I thought: "O.K., do your thing, and I will do mine, and I got on with doing some paper work with which I had got behind. After the third session spent in this way, Susie gave me one of those secret looks which I had become used to, but this time she almost shouted at me: "Aren't you ever going to talk to me?"

After this we never looked back. She became my teacher, and a very stern and demanding teacher she was, too. I could never get my letters done as well as she required or get my sums right. I had to stand in the corner and be punished by not being allowed to say anything. Eventually she softened a bit toward this retarded pupil, and we began to have some fun together and lots of laughs, when we remembered the mute Susie. I am not sure that her parents and her teachers did not sometimes wish they could go back to that phase. Susie had cured herself, just as Jan had done. She dealt with her feelings about a stern and demanding teacher by becoming even sterner and demanding of her pupil-me – and gradually a transformation took place. I used my feeling of total helplessness in the face of Susie's ability to defeat everybody to let her teach me, and we both went on to a new stage of development. This was my first and most important experience of the way counselling works and of the way in which helplessness can be used to good effect. But omnipotence can have its positive side, too.

I knew a priest at London who came to one of my groups for a short time, but he did not really fit in. He was looking for certainties and absolutes and got impatient with our searching and floundering and our rejection of absolutes. He could not see at all what we were looking for. For him everything was perfectly clear and obvious. He made me feel very helpless and frustrated because there seemed to be no possibility of any dialogue with him. We agreed to part company after a while.

Three years or later I received a report from him about the work he had started in another parish which had a large number of alcoholics, tramps, transvestites, prostitutes, addicts, promiscuous homosexuals and downs and outs.

Fred set up a service for all these people who had nothing else to turn to. At first he was available to all who cared to come for 24 hours a day. He gave them a cup of tea and sympathetic hearing. After a while he cut down for working for about 15 or 16 hours a day, but he really did provide something which was of enormous importance to many who could not use and would not come near any of our more conventional counselling services. There is a considerable measure of omnipotence in his approach, but without his certainty he could not have achieved the success he has had or inspired others to do the same. I recognize some of those feelings in myself as well. It was always a great challenge to me to take those patients off the waiting list that nobody else wanted, who were the most disturbed, the most sick, the most suicidal, the once who have been through the psychiatric mill and who had the worst prognosis. I was always willing to have a go, and since these are so often the people nobody else has ever listened to or paid much attention to, they do in fact frequently respond very well to therapy or counselling, especially in groups where they can be a great help to each other.

At first I had the mistaken idea that it all depended on me, but I soon realized that I learned more from them than they did from me. I am not quite so omnipotent now, I have experienced failure and helplessness. I am more careful in the selection of the people I take on and no longer believe that I have to be able to help everybody who comes. It was a belief I shared with many of my Clergy friends, and I now spend quite a bit of my time trying to disabuse them on this idea. There is a bit of regret there, too, though. Felling omnipotent and willing to take anything or anybody is quite exciting, even exhilarating at times, but when the inevitable fall comes it is quite a plunge.

Padraig Berard Coleman[13]

is a Catholic priest living and working in Ireland. Earlier he attended the European Conference in Lublin 1981 and gave some reports on that event

Some weeks ago I received a telephone call from London. It was Irene Bloomfield asking me to take part on this panel – could I contribute something on the theme of "Omnipotence and Helplessness of the Counsellor". At that very moment I had just returned from my rooms after a day's work feeling despondent and rather helpless. There had not been a bright moment. All the people I saw seemed unable to cope with their lives – I was beginning to feel the same! My reply to Irene was, " I will have no problem in saying something about the "helplessness" of the counsellor and I never feel omnipotent." Certainly on that evening my thinking and feeling was a long way from omnipotence. In a certain sense that summarizes what I have to say. However my old professor of philosophy would never let me away with saying "in a certain sense" – he would ask "in what sense?" hence I must elaborate.

I will take first the notion of "helplessness". In my training as a counsellor there were many occasions when I felt helpless – unable to do anything for the person in front of me. I would not know what to say. As time went on I might tentatively make some interpretation – I would think it intelligent perhaps and to the point. My client might agree – but it would not change anything. Or, I might want to do something practical – wondering whether sitting and "being with" was really enough. It was only in time that I learned and accepted that "being with" was in itself a "doing" – however difficult prolonged silence was both for the client and for myself. Confidence gradually came. Finally when I got the "piece of paper" at the end of the training I felt I had arrived. (I had completed the programme in individual, group-work and family/marital therapy). There was, I admit, a certain "inflation". That was six years ago. In that time I have been counselling continuously. In many ways and at many

---

13   This lecture was first presented at the European Conference in Turku/Finland, 1985

times I experienced the same feelings of helplessness of my years in training – I am still a "beginner".

On the day Irene phoned, among those I saw was a fourty-one year old roan, a lawyer who has never come to terms with an accident he has had nine years ago. Up to the time of his accident he was successful. Despite impairment of memory and concentration, he still yearns to be the "successful" lawyer. He wants me to help him "develop his personality" – but, without pain. He looks to me to "cure" him and says that he is still hoping for the "magic".

He was followed for the next hour by a young student counsellor of twenty seven, an only child of a very perfectionistic and obsessional mother and a strict father. She cannot cope with relationships, wears a mask to the world and wonders why when she comes to me – "I'm always crying?" She tells me that she doesn't trust me – that I have eagle eyes and that I am judging her. I sit waiting – wondering what to say, how to respond.

Finally there is a young teacher – thirty years of age; he cannot cope with the children in school, he feels inadequate and lives in fantasy – frightened by the destructive thoughts that enter his mind. He feels "weak" – looks to me for a warm relationship; and fantasies a lot about me. He is interested in astrology – he would like me to talk more about Jung and archetypes; he hopes he would have a dream which would change him. Today, he brought a dream: he is in the waiting room of a Jungian lady analyst and wonders anxiously what would I think of that …

I think these three examples of my days' work will not be unfamiliar material for anyone engaged in counselling and psychotherapy. They point up my own helplessness when confronted with people's pain: the lawyer's feelings of rejection by his partner, the young girl's sense of isolation and loneliness, the young man's poor self image and frustration. They force me to question what I am doing – whether anything is changing; whether despite training, knowledge of psychodynamics and of personality development, I too am like the ones before me. I find myself wondering whether perhaps someone else, someone more wise, more experienced, more intelligent than I (an analyst perhaps) would have had that touch which could bring order and calm into the chaos of people's lives.

It is, however, good for me to feel helpless and not to run from it. It places me along side and with my clients. I think we must experience our helplessness, even impotence, if we are to touch that part of the other that is weak, helpless and fearful – we too have our fears. To be aware of our weakness, helplessness and on occasion, even hopelessness seems essential if we are to meet "the other". Yet, there must also be the capacity to rise above such experiencing, a strength which sustains ourselves and the other as we travel the inward road of the Self.

And now the notion of "omnipotence." I have indicated that I never feel "omnipotent" – that is, I do not feel like God – having full and absolute power. It would be naive in the extreme to act as if one were God. I suggest that none of us would think of ourselves as "omnipotent" in the classical and defined sense of the word.

However, and this is something we have to grapple with constantly; we are perceived as powerful by those who come to us for help. We may dismiss this perception and knowingly call it "a projection". I am not suggesting that clients don't project such power but rather that such projections can lead to a false sense of power in us – if we collude or go along with it.

The very fact that people come seeking help inevitably puts the counsellor/therapist in a superior position. Witness their anxieties, nervousness and apprehension on meeting. I recall my meetings with a medical doctor who was rendered almost catatonic in my presence over the initial seven months of therapy. Yes, it was anxiety neurosis – and transference was operating. The fact that I did not want to be seen as "powerful" was not the issue – I was seen and perceived that way.

One aspect of "omnipotence" I would like to comment on is "control". After all we *do* set up the meeting; we decide whether we will "take" this client or not; we decide the fee; we set limits and boundaries; we can remain remote and unavailable. We even decide which way the chairs are arranged. Recently a man I have been seeing for over a year commented on the chair arrangement – he didn't like it saying: "You can observe me"... he paused and concluded – "I could change my chair of course". However, he did not do so.

All this may seem quite obvious. Yet in practice we can fail to pay attention to what for the counselee is perhaps grappling with the all-powerful, omnipotent parental figure. If I bask in being that all-powerful, omnipotent counsellor then I will keep and sustain the client in a state of infantilism. I will endorse myself as a magician. We are all open to what Guggenbuhl calls the "magician projection", I quote:

"The analyst finds it extremely difficult not to be affected by this magician projection. In fact he even stimulates in the patient by trying to stress his own power and prestige. When the patient tells him of his troubles, the analyst lets him see that he already understands everything. Through the use of certain gestures, such as a sage nodding of the head and of pregnant remarks interjected among the patient's statements, the analyst creates the impression that while he may not be prepared to communicate all his knowledge and profound thoughts, he has already plumbed the depths of the patient's soul."

While we disclaim any pretension to be "omnipotent" there is perhaps our shadow side – where we would be like to be as God. It is our own dark side which we might be unwilling to acknowledge and is perhaps lurking in the background. The unconscious can catch up on us.

We might want to make our clients see life as we do – to act "normally"; we might want to be more effective; we might wish to make them "in our image and likeness". We might wish to dominate (for the clients good, of course!): to be recognized and acknowledged both by our clients and by other professionals as being "good" (that is, effective) counsellors. This is the "omnipotent shadow" within.

Omnipotence, then, in the counsellor/therapist always needs vigilance. Such vigilance will allow us become more conscious of the shadow; it will challenge us when we attempt (if we do) to dominate, to "own", manipulate, and exercise power over others.

Few will claim "omnipotence". Yet there can be more subtle approaches: For example a collusion with the notion that we do have "the power" to change people – that we are full of insight, knowledge, wisdom. Not of course that we would say so openly! Attitudes are conveyed without verbalization. Here as in everything to do with counselling or psychotherapy, our personality affects the other.

If we are blind to the "omnipotence shadow" in ourselves, then indeed we become charlatans.

Alistair V. Campbell[14]

is one of the convenors of the first International Congress in Edinburgh 1979; Professor of Bioethics, University of Otago Medical School, Dunedin, New Zealand

The English poet, Charles Causley, has a delightful poem entitled "Ten Types of Hospital Visitor". He describes the first visitor as "entering the ward in the manner of a 930's destroyer showing the flag in the Mediterranean". The poem goes on:

> Ceaselessly firing all-purpose smiles
> At everyone present
> She destroys hope
> in the breasts of the sick
> Who realise instantly
> That they are incapable of surmounting
> Her ferocious goodwill

Of course, we will find it hard to see *ourselves* in such a person. Nurtured in non-directiveness, schooled to analyse process, forced to painful self-assessment by our own trainers or analysts, we easily see ourselves as far removed from the crusading visitor who wears (as Causley puts it in another line of the poem) the "neon armour of virtue". Not for us such patronising power, not for us such lack of perception of *our* need to be needed. I expect most of us resonate to the idea of the *helplessness* of the counsellor, but omnipotence?

---

[14] This lecture was first presented at the European Conference in Turku, Finland, 1985 and first published in: *Newsletter of the International Council on Pastoral Care and Counselling, Winter 1986*

No, surely not – that (we want to say) can be only a projection from the helped person as their "child" seeks out a parent, a projection we should allow only in order to show its unreality, its misunderstanding of what we really have to offer in counselling.

And yet, is it really quite so simple? Are we really so exempt (we products of the clinical training approach to helping) from omnipotent fantasies? But (perhaps more surprisingly) we must also ask: *can* we and *should* we be denying the power which can operate in us or through us? In this short talk I want to approach this question in a paradoxical manner, by saying both a "yes" and a "no" to the omnipotence and the helplessness of the counsellor. So the first section of my talk is entitled "On Not Taking Ourselves Too Seriously", while the second – perversely – is entitled "On Taking Ourselves With Total Seriousness". Christianity and Judaism have an important thing in common, something which is often overlooked and which, I think, sets them apart from other world religions – they produce, nourish and perpetuate *jokes*. Think of the endless fund of stories about rabbis, priests and ministers, about Protestants, Catholics and Jews, about the God seen through Christian and the God seen through Jewish eyes, about the absurdity of ritual and the dubious intentions of prayer. Of course there are amusing and paradoxical stories from other religious sources – "The Exploits of the Incomparable Mulla Nasrudin" by Idries Shah springs immediately to mind. But there is something special about Jewish and Christian religious humour. It is like the court jester at the table of the kings – it dares to question the most solemn, most powerful, most feared aspects of the religious belief. It assumes that the God of the Christians and the Jews has, in making humankind in the divine image, included in that likeness a part of divinity we call "a sense of humour". In other faiths, paradoxical statements can lead the seaker to greater wisdom. But the Jewish God *certainly* – and the Christian God *probably – enjoys a joke.*

That is why a pastoral counsellor, without a sense of humour is like a Scotsman without a bank account – in a state of anxious impotence. But the truth is that we often let our enthusiasm for the new insights which counselling training can bring totally obscure our God-given sense of humour. Like the person who gave himself 9/10 of humility we give ourselves 9/10 for insight and we fail to imagine how funny all our efforts to be really effective counsellors will look *sub specie aeternitatis*. So one kind of helplessness we could do with more of is the helplessness of mirth, of people who don't take themselves too seriously and, in seeing the futility of their efforts and the arrogance of their claim to help in quite terrible human situations, can only laugh, or cry, or more likely, both.

Ogden Nash has a memorable poem called "Experience to Let" only I cannot remember it! At least not all of it. But here are a few lines which might serve to remind us that we might train for years and years, have endless experience of supervised counselling, have mastered every new text-book, every latest fashion in human science, and *still* be crashing bores who fail to see that every new encounter is also a new beginning and, that much better than the closed mind of self-confidence, are the open hands of the vulnerable helper.

> Experience is a futile teacher
> Experience is a prosy preacher
> Experience is a fruit tree fruitless
> Experience is a shoe-tree bootless
> For utter weariance and drearience
> Depend, my boy, on experience.

So whatever our experience, we are (or should be) helpless, reduced to laughter and tears by irony that we of all people think *we* can help others. But now the other side of the paradox. For, the God with the sense of humour is also the God of thunder and storm, of dark mysterious places and deserts awesome in beauty and strangeness. Love and wrath come together in the Jewish *Jehovah* but equally in the Christian *Lamb of God*. In the phrase of Rudolf Otto, there is God mysterium *tremens et fascinans*. So pastoral counsellors have to take themselves with total seriousness and not deny the power they are called to mediate in their helping others.

The story is told of the old Scottish preacher who was delivering a sermon – as he always did – on hellfire and damnation. He was just working up the climax of his sermon, in which the tortures of the damned were graphically described – "and in that day of fire and sulphur and terrible darkness there will be weeping and wailing and gnashing of teeth" ...

Then he noticed to his fury that one member of the congregation was laughing. Pretending not to notice, he repeated weeping and wailing and gnashing of teeth. There was the laughter again – it came from an old woman sitting near the front of the congregation and as he glanced at her she opened her mouth and gleefully pointed to her bare gums – not a tooth in her head! The preacher began a third time: "In that terrible day there will be weeping and wailing and *gnashing of the teeth* – and teeth will be provided."

Such confidence in divine power and initiative is perhaps a little bit absent in our present preoccupation with skilled counselling! Because we take ourselves too seriously we fail to take ourselves seriously enough. We forget that the omnipotence of God is very different from the omnipotence which men and women sometimes fantasize they possess. Human omnipotence is a *frozen* condition – the crazy shape of the muscle-bound body-builder comes to mind – or the tragic omnipotence of nuclear stockpiling with each side's determination to have total destructive power and more. The body-builders must stay locked with pumped-up muscles, the nations caught in the arms race are totally imprisoned by remorselessness logic and mutual assured destruction. But divine omnipotence is other, quite other. We see it described by the prophets of Israel in terms of convent God pleading with his people, a God well described by Abraham Heschel as "wounded lover". And the Christian God is the God on the cross whose powerlessness is the only real power over death and evil. Divine omnipotence is a *dynamic* not a state condition. It is a use of total power to bring about change, but at great risk to a person exercising power: All *could* be lost, but that must be risked in order that *anything* can be truly won.

This dynamic way of omnipotence means that the counsellor takes with total seriousness the possibility that in a mysterious and inexplicable way, divine power to avert the evil in individual and communal life operates only in the most fallible and vulnerable of all contexts, human relationships. There is no secret channel for God's omnipotence, no hidden magic going apart from the messiness of human attempts to help, of which we pastoral counsellors are a part. That is why the British sociologist, Paul Halmos, was quite right to entitle his study of the rise of the counselling movement: "The *Faith* of the Counsellors". The evidence that counselling can really make a better life for people, that it can genuinely bring about a more humane society, such evidence is ambiguous at best, and is often simply not to be found. I have often thought that counsellors should take as their motto some words of T.S. Eliot:"We are undefeated, only in that we have gone on trying". The point is that, once we cast aside delusions of omnipotence about the effectiveness of what we do, we are then ready to be really serious, seeing in our vulnerability and uncertainty a space for one little segment of divine omnipotence – that creative move for genuine change, which religious people still hope for, despite appearances.

Edwin Muis has an extraordinary poem entitled: "The Transfiguration" which Christians may not altogether warm to, for it seems to undermine a central section of Christian belief, the eternal significance of the cross. But I read it as an exciting portrayal of what eventually it seems we all believe, as we offer to help others with our poor efforts, namely, that there is a power which can genuinely defeat the worst of evils, making it as though it had never been – a *dynamic* omnipotence. The poem portrays the renewal of all creation arⁿd finally the coming of an *un*crucified Christ.

> There he will come, Christ the uncrucified
> Christ the discrucified, his death undone
> His agony unmade, his cross dismantled
> Glad to be so – and the tormented wood
> Will cure its hurt and grow into a tree
> In a green corner springing corner of young Eden,
> And Judas damned, take his long journey backward
> From darkness into light and be a child
> Beside his mother's knee, and the betrayal
> Be quite undone and never more be done.

I feel these words speak volumes to those of us who are Christians and who seem to want to perpetuate the cross as the eternal emblem of our religion. We should instead put no boundaries on the true omnipotence of God, and dare to believe that despite our weaknesses, guilt is only a stage on the way, and, though we will never see it in its totality, the eternal power and human goodness are ultimately one.

3.2 Approaches

Ulrike Elsdörfer

In her history on the European movement on pastoral care and counselling Irene Bloomfield remarks: "It is not surprising therefore that earlier conferences dealt more with externals whilst more recent ones were concerned with deeper, more unconscious and more primitive areas of human emotions and conflicts. *Biblical themes.*"[15]

Using the stories of "Adam and Eve" and "Cain and Abel" Howard Cooper reaches the centre of these "primitive areas of human emotions and conflicts". He deals with the *basic* emotions and conflicts of mankind.

His issue is: "The persecutor/victim dynamic is one of our most universal expressions of consciousness. In an analysis of antisemitism – and particularly in an analysis of the psyche of both partners, Christians and Jews – we have a case history in collective psychotherapy with implications which reach far beyond antisemitism itself and the fate of the Jews."[16]

"My hope is that by drawing you into the mythical world of the Bible story, the feelings raised by these themes can be *contained* and *held*, as they can be contained and held and worked upon in that other mythic world

---

[15] Irene Bloomfield: The European Movement for Pastoral Care and Counselling, s. a.

[16] Howard Cooper: Persecutor and victim, s. a.

we have created for ourselves: the "sacred hour" of psychoanalysis or psychotherapy or counselling".[17]

Cooper's method of paralleling psychoanalytic insights to Jewish and Christian religious knowledge is not quite untypical for this early period of the movement of pastoral care and counselling. Depth psychology was the predominant method in European accesses to a more profound understanding of religions and their materials.

The way Cooper presents this combination is very impressive, and it relates the feelings raised by religious myths closely to the moment of bringing these in secular societies still existing feelings to the surface: in psychoanalytical therapy. Whether the "hour" of psychotherapy is "sacred", will be left open; with this remark Cooper is close to many impressions Patton[18] and others (Irene Bloomfield in her report on Assisi as well) gave: The pastoral care and counselling movement is predominantly interested in the insight in psychological dimensions, spirituality in itself is "of a different character", and sometimes it is regarded with suspicion. There exists an underlying assumption of spirituality being suppressive to the deeper psychological demands for individual freedom.

The then arising feminism has some parallels to insights of psychoanalysis. Cooper realizes these aspects. Though he mainly uses material from the Jewish history of interpretation, he is interested in "justice between man and woman", which mostly lacks in the ancient traditions as well as in the interpretation given in the Jewish and Christian history.

Cooper presents Eve in her triumph of having given birth to a child:

"Her words are in fact ambiguous. They could also be translated: "I have formed a man with God 's help "or even "I have formed a man, just like God has done". We do not know what her words mean. But we should be alerted, and disturbed, by this first ever birth. Whether the words are said in humble acceptance, or joy, or as a cry of triumph over Adam at her own

---

[17] s. a.

[18] One of the first presidents of ICPCC, editor of *The Journal of Pastoral Care*

creative powers which are like God's – and they have received all these interpretations by Jewish interpreters in the past – their effect is to deny Adam his role as the father, the co-creator of Cain. She speaks, but Adam is not acknowledged. He is excluded. In the previous chapter, in Eden, Eve has been told she will be emotionally dependent upon her husband."[19]

"Ambiguity" as well as the thoroughly treated problem of "lack of communication" within the "first family", rivalries and the children's poor acknowledgement by their parents: psychoanalysis gives an overwhelming approach to the ancient texts raised by modern societies' felt disadvantages.

Dealing with the special problem of "how to become persecutor and victim", Cooper presents a sophisticated historical survey on the psychological implications of this classical and tragic "model". The all including method of overcoming the scheme of "persecutor and victim" is a deeper and satisfactory access to communication: Cain and Abel are the negative example for this. The lack of communication leads them to murder each other.

"Cain, the victim of his mother's needs, the victim of his father's jealousy, the victim of God's revelation that we have a degree of freedom to transform our destructive passions; Cain the victim is overwhelmed by his inability to speak to his brother and in desperation invents a way out. The escape from the inability to speak *now* takes the form of the one action which will make any speech in the future impossible-murder. Victim becomes persecutor in order to escape from the need to speak, to find ways to speak, to break the silence."[20]

While "the holy hour" of psychoanalysis brings communication and a deeper insight, some forms of religious "holiness" seem to be the reason for persecution. By denying the communication with his brother Abel constitutes his own death. And this murder is a result of his brother's envy.

"You can see that we have some powerfully persecuting unconscious attitudes in Abel's denial of relatedness, in his silence, in his pursuit of ho-

---

[19] s. a.

[20] s. a.

liness at the expense of his brother. Do all victims consciously or unconsciously attract their fate?

Is there no such a thing as an *innocent* victim?"[21]

The climax of deep and valuable insights in the relation of "persecutor and victim" lies in the remark: "Oppression is the cultural possession of the oppressors."[22]

Gilah Dror presents her lecture 12 years later than Howard Cooper. She lives in Israel and not in London. The conferences already saw the encounter of Jews and Christians, building somehow a "bridge over the disastrous European history".

Howard Coopers' text is principal, concerned with "basic issues" and with then – in 1985 – still vivid bad remembrances which have to be overcome by addressing them and giving them voice. "Communication" is the key word to Coopers' lecture, and the lecture is in a touching way communicative.

Dror's lecture – though addressing general issues of mankind and working on early biblical material as "Abraham, Sarah and the first 'families'" as well – is more on an insight in "cultural" forms of counselling than aiming at a deep communication in the latter sense.

She addresses the mythical origin of Jewish and Arab/Muslim culture, by using the stories of Sarah/Isaak and Hagar/Ismael as individual stories for individual families – as the one story of Michal, who has problems mourning on her father's death, because some problems in her family are unresolved.

Dror's special contribution to the interreligious dialogue in care and counselling seems to be the information on Jewish religious tradition, as it is in a vivid practice in Israel. Care and counselling is a medium she uses for the process of opening her clients to spiritual experience in Jewish tradition. This is – perhaps – different to her predecessor, who, by means of psychotherapy and its image of man, wants to aim at "reconciliation" of former antagonists by us-

---

[21] s. a.

[22] s. a.

ing the new method of "exploring the soul and understanding its symbols".

Dror writes:

"What the rabbi uniquely brings to the counseling situation is a spiritual approach based on the wealth of Jewish tradition – texts and scriptures, history and thought – through which the search for the voice of God has traditionally taken place throughout the history of the Jewish people – a tradition which has always been aware of the ongoing struggle of the human condition – a tradition which has retained a vision of a joint partnership between humankind and God in the process of *tikun*, the ongoing process of perfecting one's self as well as the world."[23]

"Abraham's distress and subsequent failure to help brings about a positive resolution of the problem, points to the *need to maintain a calm and neutral presence in the counseling situation*. His failure to hear the nuances of God's voice serves as a reminder that one must always *search for further spiritual development and insight*. As counselors, our own religious experience colours our ability to integrate God into the counseling."[24]

In the traditional "MiShe Berach" prayer for the sick, we pray for "Refuat HaNefesh u'Refuat HaGuf" – *healing of the spirit and of the body*. In pastoral counseling we attempt to touch people's minds, and souls, in the hopes of participating in and promoting the process of healing of mind and body. This is done through the search for relevance and meaning, in which we apply our experience in studying not only counseling techniques, but also in studying rabbinic sources and hermeneutics based on critical analysis of texts and stories, to a search for deeper meanings in the stories brought to us in the counseling setting."[25]

Modern counseling and traditional spirituality – in Dror's approach they are two complementary sides of the one reality to deal with. Earlier accesses – mainly from the European presenters –, have another presupposition: that care and counselling resp. psychol-

---

[23] Gilah Dror: Riches, rivalries and responsibilities in the pastoral counseling setting

[24] s. a.

[25] s. a.

ogy/psychotherapy is able to define the implications of spiritual-ity, and that psychology has the ability to define "good" or "bad" spirituality – this seems to be a difference which has to be proved.

A certain "image of man", based on insights of psychology as Howard Cooper expressed it in his text, is one of the early antago-nists to theological anthropology (as it was formulated and used by the religious institutions in this period):

"'Sin' here are all those chaotic emotions and energies inside us that threaten our quest for wholeness, all those destructive inner forces which prevent us living to our true potential, all those unconscious urges and feelings which block or stunt our growth as human beings".[26]

The three parts of the one lecture on "Helplessness and Omnipo-tence of the Counsellor" give different approaches to their hidden subject of "projections" *(which in a way is the hidden subject of all early documents on the encounter between religion and psychology).*

Irene Bloomfield, working with children, has the best chance to bring it to the point:

"When dealing with 'helplessness and omnipotence' one has to change the image of the threatening tiger to the image of the 'laughing tiger', as one of her patients did".[27]

In her example Bloomfield presents a similar idea as Howard Cooper does: "Sin" is the unability to cope with the chaotic and elements in the unconscious (the threatening tiger) – "sin" is the unability not to transform this chaotic elements into an ability to enhance human growth: the laughing tiger in the unconscious and conscious mind.

"Taming this most savage of beasts is paralleled by the transformation of those qualities in the little girl. The reformation of the imaginary tiger has given Jannie some control over a danger which earlier had left her helpless and frightened. Another child might stalk the tiger and shoot him with his home made Tommy gun or out-roar him or become the tiger.

---

[26] Howard Cooper: Persecutor and victim., s. a.
[27] Irene Bloomflied: Helplessness and Omnipotence of the Counsellor, s. a.

These are very important experiences for the developing personality".[28]

Bloomfield's experience leads to the assumption that it is possible to learn from the child client, as she learned from her first client Susie – changing the roles of teacher and pupil, helplessness and omnipotence. By this, Bloomfield implies: changing the roles may give a fresh view on a dimension of spirituality and religion. As far as there are no such projections of passive dependence on God an active pro-creation with God is possible. With "negative" connotations Bloomfield describes her practice when dealing with one of her clients in a group:

"I knew a priest at London who came to one of my groups for a short time, but he did not really fit in. He was looking for certainties and absolutes and got impatient with our searchings and flounderings and our rejection of absolutes. He could not see at all what we were looking for. For him everything was perfectly clear and obvious. He made me feel very helpless and frustrated because there seemed to be no possibility of any dialogue with him. We agreed to part company after a while."[29]

Coleman's access is in a quite different, but as well practical way, though he reflects the relation between "helplessness and omnipotence" in a theological terminology. Here some of his practical approaches may give an easier access to his subject:

"One aspect of 'omnipotence' I would like to comment on is 'control'. After all we *do* set up the meeting; we decide whether we will 'take' this client or not; we decide the fee; we set limits and boundaries; we can remain remote and unavailable. We even decide which way the chairs are arranged. Recently a man I have been seeing for over a year commented on the chair arrangement – he didn't like it saying: 'You can observe me' ... he paused and concluded – 'I could change my chair of course'. However, he did not do so."[30]

---

[28] s. a.
[29] s. a.
[30] Padraig Berard Coleman: Helplessness and Omnipotence of the Counsellor, s. a.

Coleman's conclusion is: "If we are blind to the 'omnipotence shadow' in ourselves, then indeed we become charlatans"[31].

Not a therapeutical attitude, but an old fashioned "good character" of humans attracts *Campbell*: humour. "It assumes that the God of the Christians and the Jews has, in making humankind in the divine image, included in that likeness a part of divinity we call "a sense of humour". In other faiths, paradoxical statements can lead the speaker to greater wisdom. But the Jewish God *certainly* – and the Christian God *probably – enjoys a joke.*

That is why a pastoral counsellor, without a sense of humour is like a Scotsman without a bank account – in a state of anxious impotence."[32]

"So one kind of helplessness we could do with more of is the helplessness of mirth, of people who don't take themselves too seriously and, in seeing the futility of their efforts and the arrogance of their claim to help in quite terrible human situations, can only laugh, or cry, or more likely, both."[33]

"The God with the sense of humour is also the God of thunder and storm, of dark mysterious places and deserts awesome in beauty and strangeness. In the phrase of Rudolf Otto, there is God mysterium *tremens and fascinans.*"[34]

Campbell closes with the statement: "the eternal power and human goodness are ultimately one"[35] – thus presenting a "positive anthropology" as well as some critique on the use of too many non – productive methods and theoretical accesses, both from psychology and theology.

Bloomfield's approaches to psychology in this article seem to result from *Winnicott*[36].

Coleman remains in the theoretical – theological sphere, though reflecting "helplessness and omnipotence" as they appear in prac-

---

[31] s. a.

[32] Alistair V. Campbell: Helplessness and Omnipotence of the Counsellor, s. a.

[33] s. a.

[34] s. a.

[35] s. a.

[36] Donald W. Winnicott is a British psychoanalyst and researcher

tical settings of counseling: in the case he presents with no positive result – the client didn't change the chair (which may be result of the "shadow" of the counselling setting).

Campbell relies on "not taking too serious" all accesses, he wants to leave a "little segment of divine omnipotence – that creative move for genuine change, which religious people still hope for, despite appearances."[37]

---

[37] Alistair V. Campbell: Helplessness and Omnipotence of the Counsellor, s. a.

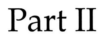
Part II

4 International Council on Pastoral Care and Counselling

Congresses

John H. Patton

ICPCC's mission:

To promote the reflective theory and practice of pastoral care and counselling throughout the world.

To inform, educate and inspire practitioners of pastoral care and counselling in various contexts in the world.

To enable practitioners of pastoral care and counselling to be resources
for one another and to learn from each other's cultures, traditions and
practices.

To support and advocate for the unique and essential dimension of
spirituality in the teaching and practice of pastoral care and counselling.

To develop relevant theories in the field of pastoral care and counselling and to this end to engage in interdisciplinary discourse.

To organize and assist in organizing of conferences, consultations and
meetings in various areas of the world.

To support the development of counselling centres and organizations
for pastoral care and counselling in various parts of the world.

To increase interaction with other care and counselling organizations.

4.1 Religion's and psychology's encounter in cura animarum

*John H. Patton, the vice-president of the first International Congress in Edin-
burgh 1979, gives a comment in an editorial of the "Journal of Pastoral Care"[1]
His and Don Browning's articles are the contributions to care and counselling
from an American point of view*

4.1.1 Documents

4.1.1.1 The International Pastoral Care and Counseling Movement: What Is it?

John H. Patton

---

[1] *The Journal of Pastoral Care*, Vol. XXXVII, June 1983, No. 2, p. 81-83

"I must acknowledge from the outset that I cannot really answer the question posed by the title of this editorial. For some time I have been searching for the international movement's organizing principle, internal dynamic, or even the boundaries between what it is and is not. There are a number of important features of the movement, some of which I touch here, but as yet it is difficult to go beyond the image used by the Dutch pastoral theologian, Heije Faber, who once described the international movement as 'an invisible community'.

Ten years ago, in an issue of *The Journal*, Charles Stewart expressed the hope that *The Journal of Pastoral Care* would, to some degree at least, become an international journal with regular contributions from many countries. That hope has not been realized. We have in the last ten years received very few articles from outside North America. Certainly, that is bad news for those of us in the United States and Canada who have not had the opportunity to read such material. I believe, however, that it also reflects the good news that persons from other parts of the world are only marginally interested in reporting to the "mother country" of modern pastoral care what they are doing. Their primary interest lies in communicating among themselves and developing their own region of the world.

The organizing principle of the international pastoral care and counselling movement, then, is not really a principle or even a method of learning. It is a community of people from many places of religious ministry who have been learning to listen to and share what is happening to them in the deeper experience of human life. It is dialogue across many different types of boundaries about the ministry of caring and our own experiences of being cared for ".[2]

"CPE, however, is not the international movement's organizing principle. The British, for example, are very careful to say that their clinical training is not CPE …

Another common, or almost common, concern in the International Pastoral Care and Counseling movement is with practice of some kind of interpersonal ministry. Probably most participants in the conference are still clergy, but the place of ordination in the practice of this ministry differs widely in relation to the various contexts, countries and confessions

---

[2]   John H. Patton, in: The International Pastoral Care and Counseling Movement: What Is It?, In: *The Journal of Pastoral Care, p. 81*

where it is practiced. The word 'pastoral', for example, means several different things. Does it primarily represent caring attitudes and acts or administrative oversight by a responsible clergyperson? Depending upon confessional tradition, it may mean one or the other or both. Because of this multiple meaning, the term pastoral may not be the best word to describe what we are; but we have not yet come up with a more accurate one. We can only conclude that the international movement has been consistently concerned with the caring ministry of religious communities, but a fully satisfactory way of describing this has not yet been developed.

For some time I felt that the interest or concern shared internationally, was "the living human document" – the case ...

An interest in psychology is another common theme. Some of those involved actively in international conferences are psychologists and non-medical psychoanalysts. Psychological language is in common usage and because of its commonality is sometimes quickly recognizable from one language to another. Psychological and psychotherapeutical theory is a major element in the discussion between persons from different countries. The Americans and Germans may discuss Kohut together. Some listen with expectation when the British talk about Klein and Winnicott. Freud and Jung seem to offer a common point of discussion for almost everyone. Most participants in the international movement are religious professionals who believe that psychological knowledge can contribute both to our apprehension of our faith and the practice of it. We differ, however, in many ways in our understanding of the degree and ways that this is the case; but most of us can speak to each other in "psychology".

The "psychology" we speak is most often therapeutic psychology. Throughout the world people seem to be interested in counseling, whether it is spelled with one "l" or two. The International Committee on Pastoral Care and Counselling maintains the term counseling in its title. This suggests that counseling, understood in some way, is an important part of the international scene. The central concerns of the American Association of Pastoral Counselors, however, seem to be unique to the United States and Canada. Integrating pastoral counseling with ministry and theology seems relatively unimportant to the rest of the world. Indeed there are many pastors who do some type of pastoral counseling and clergy who practice Jungian or psychoanalytic psychotherapy, AAPC's affirmation that psychotherapy can be an appropriate expression of pastoral min-

102

istry is our thing, not theirs. Also peculiar to North America is the belief of some of us that in the pastoral counseling centre we have developed a new form of the church in the world – a way of reaching persons untouched by traditional religious congregations. There is genuine international dialogue about pastoral care, clinical pastoral education, and psychological theory; but thus far the dialogue about counseling centres and pastoral psychotherapy is almost exclusively an American one. Although there is an international interest in counseling, it is in such a variety of forms that dialogue about it is sometimes difficult".[3]

By explaining CPE theory and method the access is given to the differences between American pastoral care and counselling and the primarily psychoanalytical theories and methods deriving from European origin in the practice of counselling in religions' contexts. CPE – Clinical Pastoral Education – is the genuine method of caring and counselling as it emerged after Boisen and Howard Clinebell in the USA.
Later on systemic approaches to therapy as well as humanistic psychology had their main fundaments in the USA as well, but they soon spread to many other countries.
Speaking of the religions' accesses to psychotherapy and counselling in this realm means: The Jewish and Christian access to these methods and practices. As Patton writes:

"The organizing principle of the international pastoral care and counselling movement, then, is not really a principle or even a method of learning. It is a *community of people* from many places of religious ministry who have been learning to listen to and share what is happening to them in the deeper experiences of human life. It is a *dialogue across many different types of boundaries* about the ministry of caring and our own experiences of being cared for. Most of the persons involved share the Judeo-Christian tradition and practice and reflect upon their ministry in the light of that tradition."[4]

---

[3]   John H. Patton: The International Pastoral Care and Counseling Movement: What Is It?, In: *The Journal of Pastoral Care, p. 82*
[4]   John H. Patton: The International Pastoral Care and Counselling Movement: What Is it?, in: *The Journal of Pastoral Care, p. 84*

Don S. Browning

The following lecture reflects on the background of the Judeo-Christian tradition. Accesses to natural sciences, to philosophy and politics as well as to theology from American and European origin present the state of the interdisciplinary discussion concerning the relations between care and counselling and psychotherapy, and concerning the encounter of psychology and religion in the 1970s and 1980s.

4.1.1.2   Citizenship, Saintliness and Health.
The Relations of Religion and the Clinical Psychological Disciplines

Don S. Browning[5]

then Alexander Campbell Professor of Religion and Psychological Studies at The Divinity School, University of Chicago.

The emerging situation of competition between psychiatry and religion is probably more exacerbated today than it was from 1940 to the 1970's. During this period, there were significant areas in American society where the religion and the clinical psychological disciplines developed various kinds of friendly relations and alliances. The liberal Protestant theological establishment from the 1930's to the present, in the United States and Western Europe, has spawned a variety of authors and organisations that tried to develop a working friendship between liberal Christianity and the clinical psychological disciplines. In the writings of Anton Boisen, Reinhold Niebuhr, Paul Tillich, David Roberts and Seward Hiltner and a host of organizations such as the American Association of Pastoral Counselors and the Association of Clinical Pastoral Education, various efforts were made to develop a cooperative and non-competitive relation between religion and clinical psychology and

---

[5]   This lecture was delivered by Prof. Don Browning in Edinburgh on Nov. 7th 1979 as "Margaret Allen Lecture". Margaret Allen was a deaconess of the Church of Scotland being interested in psychotherapy. She was the founder of the Scottish pastoral association. Published in: *Contact. 1990: 2*. The lecture was shortened by Ulrike Elsdörfer

psychiatry. In these liberal Protestant quarters, the strategy was per-spectival rather than synthetic or triumphalist. By this I mean, these theologians and groups held that clinical psychology and psychi-atry were valid, although not exhaustive, perspectives of human behaviour. There were other perspectives on human behaviour as well, and these voices held that theology was one of these valid per-spectives. For instance, as Tillich said, religion addresses existential anxiety, real guilt, and faith as the answer to these universal human problems. On the other hand, the clinical psychologies, he claimed, address issues in neurotic anxiety, unrealistic guilt, mental illness and mental health. The categories of illness and health (the province of psychiatry) were distinguished by Tillich from the categories of real guilt and faith (the province of religion). Although it was rec-ognized that in real life these provinces are never easily separable, the attitude in liberal Protestant circles was that clinical psychol-ogy and religion could help one another as long as neither stepped too far beyond their respective perspectives and meddled signifi-cantly in the special concentrations of the other. The institutional symbol of this detente was the establishment of Divinity Schools. In effect, what was happening in those days was the development of the assumption that religion could use some of the insights of the clinical psychological disciplines to help the religious response to individuals with problems in living. Even then, the Protestant reli-gious establishment knew that although psychiatry too was inter-ested in problems in living, its primary focus was on mental illness. Although these liberal Protestant churches did not want to ignore mental illness, they were quite happy to relinquish primarily initia-tives in this area to psychiatry and related clinical disciplines.

The present scene, however, is far more complex. A conversa-tion that once was dominated by liberal Protestant theologians and clinicians has now been broadened to include liberal Catholics and Jews. In addition, conservatives and fundamentalists of all faiths are now deeply into the conversation with the modern clinical psy-chologies. Furthermore, various syntheses between Jungian and hu-manistic psychology with both traditional Christianity and the so-called "new religions" are now powerful forces in our American society. In fundamentalist groups, the friendly relation that has existed between secular psychiatry and the liberal Protestant establishment does not exist.

The recent intensification of the competition between religion and the clinical psychiatric disciplines calls for new attention to the development of a public philosophy articulating psychiatry's attitude toward religion. This work is primarily a philosophical task and must be accepted as a responsibility on the part of both parties. If psychiatry is to reach out toward religion, psychiatry must be able both to define its own boundaries with greater clarity and state philosophically more empathetic and differentiated views of religion. But a similar task awaits religious leaders as well. They must be able to state, with reference to psychiatry, the special focus and limits of their religious goals and especially their religious counselling. Both psychiatry and religion must accept responsibility for articulating a public philosophy of their relation to one another. Without such a public philosophy about their mutual relation, psychiatry can inadvertently force religious bodies into an increasingly more reactionary and defensive posture, and religion can increasingly assert itself into areas of human brokenness which it must address but not completely by itself.

So the modern clinical psychologies move into various arrangements of competition and complementarity with religion because, more than they realize, they carry within them quasi-religious metaphors. They carry with them images of trust or distrust in the deep possibilities of the world that science alone can neither give us nor justify. Some will explain the phenomenon from the hermeneutic perspective and say that they contain these world images because they emerged out of religio-cultural contexts and still carry these heritages secretly in their inner recesses of their theoretical models. Others will say that they project these quasi-religious myths and symbols out of whatever humble materials they are given. The clinical psychological and psychiatric disciplines, for good or ill, may have become endowed with religious overtones, not always because this has been imposed on them by religionists, but because the clinical disciplines themselvs have not been able to maintain their boundaries with complete scientific purity. Nor is it clear that as practical endeavors actively involved in the process of treatment these disciplines can ever aspire to arrive at such total scientific purity.

So, where do we go from here?

My view is that the clinical psychological disciplines must acknowledge their practical and value-laden character. This means that the natural science model of the clinical psychological and psychiatric disciplines must be repudiated as the dominant philosophy of these disciplines. To say this, of course, does not mean that there are no natural science submoments within these disciplines. But to acknowledge that there are natural science submoments within them does not itself justify making the natural science model exhaustive of their total reality as practices. Furthermore, this should not be seen as an embarrassment but as an opportunity for the psychiatric disciplines to make a new alliance with philosophy and ethics that would facilitate the formulation of a public philosophy governing their relation with religion.

In the remaining time, let me list a few general principles that might contribute to such a public philosophy. In presenting this brief summary, I will be putting forward some of the central ideas of two volumes I am editing composed of essays written by psychiatrists, ethicists, theologians, and historians on the question of the need for a public philosophy to govern the relation of psychiatry and religion. Larson's call for a closer relation of psychiatry and religious institutions is important, but it is not likely to happen until the fundamental philosophical principles governing such cooperation are clearer in the minds of all participating parties.

The clinical psychological disciplines and religion should be differentiated from one another, as indeed for the most part they have been in western societies over the last several decades. But this differentiation does not necessarily mean total and complete separation. There have been and will continue to be various lines of overlap, analogy, and mutual influence between psychiatry and religion. This is understandable, inevitable, and useful.

Although there are overlaps each has its distinct focus. The clinical psychiatric disciplines are interested in health, and religion – especially western religion – is interested primarily in self-transcendence. By self-transcendence, I mean the capacity to focus one's energies beyond the self for the good of the other. There is nothing that prevents the clinical psychological and psychiatric disciplines either from studying self-transcendence and the technical means to achieve it. What keeps the modern clinical psychologies from studying and promoting self-transcendence are the structures of functioning within the constraints of two interacting principles, i.e., the idea of the separation of church and state is characteristic of the social philosophy of most modern pluralistic societies and the related idea that all science should be value free.

In reality these disciplines are not values free. At the least, they are in the service of the value of mental health. But mental health itself is never definable or thinkable independently of other more positive images of human fulfilment. Since, in American pluralistic society no single positive definition of human fulfilment, and certainly no single definition of self-transcendence, can gain total public approval, the clinical disciplines rightly attempt to find the widest common value to serve, i.e. some roughly defined concept of health, as difficult as it is both to conceptualize or to abstract from other values.

In spite of the fact that psychiatry and related disciplines serve the value of health and religion serves primarily the value of self-transcendence, they still may have important supportive and critical functions to play for one another. The clinical psychological disciplines have been useful in critiquing certain forms of religion and self-transcendence that seemed harmful to the values of health. This should be seen as a useful contribution to religion. On the other hand, it is not entirely clear that mental health is a value that can stand by itself or be achieved by pursuing it alone. In situations of unhealth and imbalance, it may require the capacity for self – transcendence and self – sacrifice on the part of some individuals in order to return a situation of imbalance to health. Hence, the clinical psychiatric and psychological disciplines may actually have an investment in religion's capacity to form some individuals in soci-

108

ety to have considerable capacity for self-transcendence and self-sacrifice. This is simply to say that for psychiatry to do its work in supporting and enhancing mental health, it may need to recognize the need for healthy and balanced religious institutions to do their work of promoting self-transcendence as well.

Although religion and the clinical psychiatric disciplines always will to some extent overlap, their real point of meeting is around the concept of citizenship. The concept of health can never be defined without reference to some understanding of the kind of society we live in and the minimal social, work, and interpersonal skills needed for function in such a society. If this is so, the clinical psychological disciplines must develop their images of health in close association with those disciplines working to define normative models of citizenship in liberal democratic societies. The well-known social psychologist Brewster Smith made the same point nearly fifteen years to accomplish the goals of human growth and fulfillment. But they cannot, without the help of the normative sciences, tells us what these goals should be. Even if we define health as the capacity to act with some degree of freedom, this capacity can never be concretely defined without reference to the positive values that this capacity actually serves. Hence, either directly or indirectly the clinical psychological disciplines need to be in conversation with the normative disciplines of political science and moral philosophy.

The philosophy of religion, however, also should make a contribution to a philosophy of psychiatry. Citizenship requires models of self-transcendence. Models of democratic citizenship require models of self-transcendence and self-sacrifice that have been the contribution of the special religious traditions, both Christian and Jewish, in our society. Concepts of citizenship may be the mediating concept between health as the special interest of the clinical psychiatric disciplines and self-transcendence as the special interest of religion. The special foci of these cultural interests require a vital interaction and mutual enrichment. This requires that the specialists of the disciplines of psychology, politics, and religion remain in active conversation with one another. The dotted lines that permit the relative autonomy of these disciplines should not become absolute walls of separation. Models of health, citizenship, and saintliness must continue to nourish one another for the common good.

4.2 Approaches

Ulrike Elsdörfer

Browning's article addresses the main issues being discussed by many researchers in the field of psychology and religion in these times. There are no special comments on the article necessary.

To follow the logic Browning uses in his arguments, here some extracts:

1. Various efforts were made to develop cooperative and non-competitive relations between religion and clinical psychiatry.
2. The modern clinical psychologies move into various arrangements of competition and complementarities with religion because, more than they realize, they carry with them quasi religious metaphors.
3. The clinical psychological disciplines and religion should be differentiated from one another, as indeed for the most part they have been separated in western societies over the last several decades. But this differentiation does not necessarily mean total and complete separation. There have been and will continue to be various lines of overlap, analogy, and mutual influence between psychiatry and religion. This is understandable, inevitable, and useful.
4. Although there are overlaps each has its distinct focus. The clinical psychiatric disciplines are interested in health, and religion – especially western religion – is primarily interested in self-transcendence. By self-transcendence, I mean the capacity to focus one's energies beyond the self for the good of the other.
5. The clinical psychological disciplines must acknowledge their practical and value-laden character. This means that the natural science model of the clinical psychological and psychiatric disciplines must be repudiated as the dominant philosophy of these disciplines.
6. The philosophy of religion, however, also should make a contri-

bution to a philosophy of psychiatry. Models of democratic citizenship require models of self-transcendence and self-sacrifice that have been the contribution of the special religious traditions, both Christian and Jewish, in our society. Concepts of citizenship may be the mediating concept between. This requires that the specialists of the disciplines of psychology, politics, and religion remain in active conversation with one another".[6]

Browning's reflections are based on concepts of western psychology and psychotherapy, on "western religions" (Jewish and Christian) and on the special way western societies regard their cultural and religious traditions. An access to the self-presentation of indigenous religions and to the reflection on non-western religions, according to their present state in the 1980's and 1990's, will be introduced in the following texts.

---

[6]   Don S. Browning: Citizenship, saintliness and health, s. a.

5 Intercultural and interfaith encounter

Wholeness and healing as well as the all-including assumption of sacredness and sanctity are the underlying conceptions of the following contributions: the speakers and writers explain their religious traditions; by encountering the questions of caregivers they offer an insight in their backgrounds from their individual cultural and religious roots.

In the previous chapters there were adressed the two religions of Judaism and Christianity, concerning their common roots. Their members shared geographical and in many cases social spheres in history.

As the common tradition of these two religions mostly implies equal social standards of their members in modern and "western" societies (including Israel), members of other religions than Judaism and Christianity have a quite different access to care and counselling regarding their geographical and historical situations. Care and counselling for them is deriving from many implications of "western" lifestyle, coming with colonialization, as it was the case for Asian Budhist and Hindu culture as well as for many people from parts of the world dominated by Islamic traditions.

An encounter of these religions with methods and world-views of psychotherapy and counselling has to consider the social differenciation between the societies they derive from. Indigenous world-views, as the Canadian First Nations' contribution shows, address social marginalization after colonization.

The encounter of religions and clinical methods necessarily has to be an encounter in individuals' daily attitudes and accesses to life, in order to profoundly understand the world in which the different partners live. The following contributions approach various religions in their attitude towards the individual's life in its special traditions and its spiritual dimensions: concerning the religious and therapeutical issues of "wholeness" and "healing", as well as the religious aspects of "sacredness".

Islamic and Buddhist accesses predominantly are driven by ethics: achieving peace in order to preserve the creation is the Islamic advice,

113

meditation, awareness, "mindfulness" for every action and experience is the Buddhist recommendation.

5.1 Documents

5.1.1 Islam Stories for Transition in a Strange Land

Fuad Sahin[1]

is a medical doctor of Turkish origin then living in Niagara Falls, Canada. At the time of this lecture he is the President of the Council of the Muslim Community in Canada.

Pastoral care means counselling and advising regarding religious matters. This is done in churches, homes, hospitals, nursing homes and similar institutions.

Baptizing the new-born, solemnizing marriages, visiting the sick, praying for the distressed and ministering to the dying all fall into pastoral care.

Similar services are rendered by the Muslim clergyman, whom we call Imam, but not as formally as within the Christian Tradition. Since Islam does not recognize a special institution for the clergy; any person with adequate knowledge and experience could fulfill these functions. Islam places emphasis on direct communication between the individual and God. Intercession is forbidden.

In Muslim countries the Government has a Ministry of Islamic Affairs responsible for matters such as running schools; to graduate Islamic scholars, taking care of mosques and providing them with Imams. The Imams lead the regular daily prayers; give sermons; answer questions pertaining religion, solemnize marriages, and conduct funeral services. Teaching of the Qu'ran, the Holy Book of Islam is also provided in some mosques. In countries where moslems

---

[1]   A lecture delivered in Toronto/Canada, 1995, in: James Reed: Babylon and Jerusalem. Stories for Transition in a Strange Land

are a minority, mosques provide Islamic education for children and adults, daily or on weekends. The Imams in such countries are appointed by the local Muslim community who also pays his salary and controls his performance. The Imam is assisted in his duties by volunteers from the community.

In Muslim Countries, the Minister of Religious Affairs provides special offices in different districts of the country to supervise the proper function of the mosques. These offices are headed by a senior scholar who is qualified to answer difficult, complicated questions and solve any problems. The Ministry also runs the religious courts in cooperation with the Ministry of Justice.

Qu'ran is the Constitution. A body of Muslim scholars watches that the laws of the land are in accordance with the Qu'ran and the Sunnah which is the teaching and tradition of the prophet Muhammad.

Conflicts between the state and the religious body are not uncommon. Scholars may differ on resolving certain religious issues. Such disagreements are not always solved amicably. Unfortunately they may end up in violent confrontation, as we are witnessing recent events in some Muslim countries.

Since all religions are interested in the well-being of mankind this purpose is defeated if they cause conflict, injustice and violence. It is very saddening to a truly religious person to see people of the same religion attack each other.

Man has not come on planet earth by his own choice. He is here for a purpose. Only religion recognizes this fact and defines this purpose. It is to serve the creator. Serving God starts with the recognition and acknowledgement of the existence of God, caring for, and loving all creation. The purpose of religion is to provide peace. Peace among humans; peace between man and all living things; peace between man and his environment.

Man has constantly misunderstood religion, distorted it, misused it and demeaned it. Right are those who claim that more people have been killed and are still being killed all over the world in the name of religion than for any other reasons. Man has the potential of turning the world into a happy place. He is the recipient of the magic gift of love, intellect, sense of reponsibilities and the natural inclination to do good, uphold justice and abhor injustice, destruction and violence. What makes man act against his own nature and turn himself into a selfish, arrogant, violent and destructive tyrant? This should be the most important subject for study by all humans; particularly of those who confess religion. Identifying the causes and prescribing the remedies has been done again and again over the long history of mankind through all religions but man has constantly failed to learn; he kept repeating the same mistakes again and again. In the past, man's capacity to destroy was small; the damages he caused were limited in population, space and time. Over the last fifty years man has acquired the means and capacity to destroy the entire planet. We are causing the death of millions of humans through wars, massacres, uprooting people from their lands and homes, causing diseases through the use of fertilizers, inscecticides, pesticides, freon, chlorine, PCB's and many other chemicals.

We are destroying the physical body as well as the mind of millions through the use of tobacco, alcohol, and a multitude of other drugs. We are causing the extermination of many living species everyday. We are polluting rivers, lakes, oceans and subterranean waters. We are polluting the air we breathe, destroying the forests which purify the air and provide oxygen besides sheltering millions of different living species, animal and vegetable. The ozone layer of the upper atmosphere which protects us against the harmful solar rays is also disappearing because of wrongdoing.

Nature is resilient: it will change, adapt and survive as bacteria and viruses are adapting, resisting and surviving the most sophisticated antibiotics. Man may not be as smart as the bacteria and viruses. His knowledge and experience may not prevent his extinction. He may however, take pride that he is the master: that not only has he the capacity of destroying everything, but he also has the means and the power of destroying himself. Unfortunately, after he is gone nobody will erect a monument in recognition of his accomplishments.

It is incumbent on every human being to do something to avert the ultimate tragedy. People of faith are well-equipped and well-placed to lead. They should join hands and work together at every level of the society: in families, schools, farms, factories, universities, governments. (They should) work with women and men, young and old, rich and poor in order to get the message loud and clear and mobilize all means to make the world a good place to live in and to prevent a great tragedy.

5.1.2   Buddhist Stories for Transition in a Strange Land

Suwanda H. J. Sugunasiri[2]

is born in Sri Lanka and immigrated to Canada. Ph.D. in education from the University of Toronto

Introduction

Sisters and brothers in spirituality, I want to thank you for inviting me to share with you some stories and thoughts from the Buddhist perspective on the topics of this conference, "Transition in a Strange Land". Some of you have traveled far to be with us today, and we are deeply honoured that we get an opportunity to meet with you and learn from the rich experience you bring to this conference. I know it to be way more than my own limited experience. You deal with the rough and the tumble, and I want to congratulate you on the excellent job you are doing under tying conditions. It is my hope that what I have to say adds a bit to your wide conceptual world, but if I have failed to do even that little, I seek indulgence, understanding and compassion.

We have one whole hour to be together, and so I thought that before you go to sleep on me as I drone on you should at least know what you are going to miss! So I will give you a synopsis first. I

---

2   A lecture delivered in Toronto/Canada, 1995. Shortened by Ulrike Elsdörfer. In: James Reed: Babylon and Jersualem. Stories for Transition in a Strange Land

begin with the Enlightenment story of the Buddha, one, I am sure, only too familiar to you. Following that, we will relate the story of the pathological mindbody, from the Buddhist point of view, the one you have to deal with day in day out using metaphysical analysis as well. We will conclude with the healing story of that pathological mindbody, introducing you to the practice of meditation as well.

The Enlightenment Story of the Buddha

But what relevance has the Buddha story to pastoral care? The relevance is that he has a message, and a practice, of healing. It is not without reason, as we shall see, that he was known in his own life time as "the Great Physician" *(mahosadha)*, a particular text even listing a *materia medica* if items sanctioned by the Buddha for the purpose of physical healing. Indeed in one of his previous brith he was born as Mahosadha the Wise, having been born with a medicine in hand, earning the label "medicine child". Continuing the tradition, later Mahayana Buddhism has developed concepts such as "Boddhisatvas of Healing" and even a "healing Buddha". A contemporary therapist in the US, discussing the Buddha in relation to Freud, calls him Dr. Buddha.

But who is the Buddha? I shall introduce his story. Born in Lurnbini in current Nepal in 566 BCE as Prince Siddharta Gautama to Queen Mahayama and King Suddhodana, he married at the age of sixteen to Yaodhara. As was benefitting a prince, he lived a life of luxory, in his three seasonal palaces, "enjoying the pleasures of the sense" as he puts it in his own words! But encountering a different kind of reality in the form of a sick person, an old one, a dead one and a wandering ascetic (of which there were many in Siddharta's India), set him through a process of reflection. The outcome was drastic. Here's the Buddha telling his own story:

"After some time, being young, a boy, black-haired, endowed with goody-outh, in the first period of life, although my parents were unwilling and weeping, with tears on their faces, I set forth from home to homelessness, shaving off my hair and beard and dressing in brown clothes."

The immediate catalyst for the reunification was the birth of their only offspring, Son Rahula.

Upon taking to the new path, the wandering ascetic 'Gautama' learns at the feet of two highly spiritual masters of the time, Arada Kalama and Uddaka Ramaputra by name. His mastery of what they had to offer was so complete that he is invited by both of them to take on co-leadership, but turning them down politely, he leaves them, in pursuit of a solitary search. "Meditation at night: I inititated energy, undeterred, attended to self-possession, not distracted, calmed my body, not excited, and concentrated my thoughts, focused on one point."

See on after the Buddha gives his very first expose of what he has had experienced and discovered at the Deer Park in Sanarath. For the next 45 years, we find the Buddha teaching, helping seekers of all walks of life on to the spiritual path discovered by him, engaging in spiritual debate, staving off at least one war, and ministering to the sick and needy.

To end the story of the Buddha's life, then, we see him now lying on a bed, between two trees in the Upavartana Wood near Kusina-gari. He is lying on his right side, with one foot resting on the other, self-possessed and conscious:

"Then the master adressed the monks: "Well now, monks, I am addressing you. The forces have the nature of cessation. You should succeed, through care."

This was the last speech of the thus-gone. Then the master attained the first meditation. Coming out from the first he attained the second meditation, ... third meditation, ... fourth, ... sphere of the infinity of space, and coming out from the sphere of the infinity of space, he attained the second meditation ... third meditation ... fourth, ... sphere of the infinity of space, ... sphere of the infinity of consciousness, ... sphere of nothingness, ... sphere of neither perception nor non-perception. Coming out from that he attained the cessation of the experience of perception.

Then the Buddha comes out from that and continues through the attainments and meditations in reverse order to the first meditation, then back through second and third to the fourth.

"Coming out from the fourth meditation, the master immediately attained extinction."

This is the Buddha story in brief. We close this story of Enlightenment with the observation that the Buddha both attained enlightenment and passed away in meditation.

The Four Noble Truths

It was observed that Enlightenment constituted at the highest level the discovery of the Four Noble Truths.

The First Noble truth is Suffering. Without going into its detailed psychological analysis, we'll simply take in its meaning of ordinary suffering: falling ill and dying, separation from loved ones and having to live with unloved ones, not getting what one wants, and so on.

Then there is "cessation", which means the ending of the life-cycle, the *nibhana, or,* as familiar to western folklore, Nirvana. There is a reciprocal relationship between the two. Again, without going into its psychological anlysis, we move to "the path". By this is simply meant how to bring about cessation of suffering.

Even without a detailed analysis, it will be evident that this very foundational teaching is based in a medical analogy: the condition of illness, the cause for it, its treatment and resulting wellness. This renders the Four Noble Truths as healing paradigms as well.

The Story of the Pathological Mindbody

We now explore the Buddhist understanding of the pathology of the mind, drawing upon one of the many analyses, the most relevant perhaps to a pastoral care context.

The Ailing Mindbody

The main theoretical insight we glean from the Buddha on the topic is that everything about being human is mind-based. A verse in the

Dhammapada, well-known for its succinct teachings encapsulated in poetic from, makes it amply clear:

> Mind is the forerunner, foremost it is, mindbased every-
> thing is.
> Something said or done with a good mind,
> happiness follows, like the shadow that never parts com-
> pany.
> Mind is the forerunner, foremost it is, mindbased every-
> thing is.
> Something said or done with a bad mind,
> pain follows, like the wheels the feet of the oxen.

Now, if everything is mindbased, then there are both "whole-some"(kusala), or healthy, mental concomitants of the mind, and those that are "unwholesome" (akusala), or what could be called "pathological". Our interest here, however, is not the refined break-down of these basic groups, but rather the 3-way breakdown of the mind in terms of character, wholesome or unwholesome. On the pathological side, then, they are *greed* (lobha), *anger* (dosa) and *delusion* (moha), with "non-greed", "non-anger" and "non-delusion", of course, being their wholesome counterparts.

If the mind can be called a nucleus, to fall back on science, it and the unwholesome character blemishes can be together called a "pathological mind cell".

Each of the blemishes is in a two-way relationship with the mind. That is to say first that "greed" is an archetypical constituent in the mind nucleus. So with anger and delusion. When active, each of them serves to transform the mental direction towards pathology.

The soul (given by God) or "ego", "self" or "I"(secular con-structs), is conceived by us as an unchanging permanent entity that holds one together, keeps one from falling apart and driving us into our actions and the like. But, of course, we know from science that change is the reality of all phenomena, the Buddha capturing it in the term *anicca*, literally im-permanent. Each of us, like other an-imals, plants, rocks, oceans, air and so on, is made of atoms and molecules, and they have the nature of "coming to be and passing away", having had a life of but a mind-moment. The mind, too, is a flow, a "stream of consciousness", as the Buddha characterized it.

If this understanding is correct, that means first that there simply cannot be anything, nothing indeed, that is not subject to the natural law of change. Yet we continue to believe in an unchanging, unflowing phenomenon.

The second problem is with the concept of souls from the first. It splits as under the mindbody into a duality – a changing entity called body and an unchanging one called mind. This is a difficult logic for one to understand since our mind, be it understood as "raw sensation" or as a resulting "consciousness" has to be embodied, that is to say, be based in a body. And so, if the body, namely the atoms and the molecules, change, it is impossible that something based in such body doesn't change.

The difficulty with such duality is that we are led to believe that there is on the one hand a physical manifestation, or action, and then there is an agent manifesting it, a doer doing the doing. That is to say that my talking to you now is done by somebody.

The ailing mindbody can be characterized as one in which delusion runs amok, taking greed and anger in its way.

We're all in it together

> We have seen above that greed, anger and delusion are archetypical.
> Murder or robbery are potentially waiting to manifest in each of us.
> So the primary tool is *meditation* – to overcome the archetypical blemishes.
> A Buddhist would offer as the primary tool *meditation* – even to pastoral care.
> *"For the mind is the forerunner".*

Sitting for Healing

I am sure that everyone in this August audience is adept at taking control of their mind, but you invite me to join me at this stage to get a taste of the Buddhist approach to mind cultivation.

While there are any number of meditation techniques the Buddhist world has developped over the last two and a half millenia, Zen and Tibetan to name perhaps the two best known in the west, what we are going to experience today is what the Buddha says he practiced, and claimed to be the only way to liberation. It is called "mind-ness", and is made up of two parts, "calming" and "insight". The two can run concurrently, or one after the other, but in general, calming precedes "insight".

The basic technique in mindfulness meditation is really very simple. Breathing is something we all do naturally. To "meditate", then, in the Buddhist sense is simply to *be aware* of that process of the in-flow and the out-flow of the breath. The practice thus earns the name "mindful breathing". Nothing fancy, easy and simple! That is, of course, until you try it! The nature of the mind is to turn around. You are away from home, and my mentioning that fact alone is enough to take you back to your home. Or to any other place, event, thing or person in your life, recent or in the distant past. So as one begins to calm one's mind, and to concentrate on the process of breathing, these pleasant and unpleasant memories come darting to the forefront. But paying attention to the breath, however, does not mean that you try to push darting to the forefront. But paying attention to the breath, does not mean that you try to push these out. That would be not to take your attention away from those memories. Instead what we do is pay attention to the mental intruder, gently, and invite yourself back for your focus on the breathing. We continue to focus on it as it goes in and out, not controlling, but simply observing. Like a gate keeper. He watches tall and short, fat and thin, ugly and pretty people go past him. But he neither follows them, nor does he get attached to them! He simply stays put in one place, and watches them come and go. In our meditation, too, we focus on the gate, the spot that the air passes through. This is the *tip of the nostril*. From this vantage point, we watch the now of the breath again, not following, or controlling, simply observing, observing, observing …

With these few introductory remarks, I invite you to sit comfortably in your seat, head up with neck straight, back straight, too, without leaning against the backrest and feet together.

Mindfulness meditation exercise

When we sit for long hours, we get tired. So the walking meditation is an alternative to sitting/breathing meditation, but, of course, the goal is still the same: mindfulness. In this walking meditation, we walk slowly, as slow as your body and balance would allow. Again, we keep our body straight with neck slightly tilted down to allow a 45 degree focus on the door. As we lift our foot, we say to our mind "lift" and "move" as it moves. As we keep it on the ground, we say "heel" and then "toes" following the sequence of keeping your foot. By the time your one foot is on the ground, the heel of the other foot will be on the ground, but the toes still touching the ground. And you lift it once the other foot is firmly on the ground. This, of course, is the natural way we walk. So again, we are not forcing a walk but simply watching our walk, to goal, of course, being to train the mind to stay focused.

Walking meditation exercise

We end with a few final remarks about meditation. We have a time and a place for eyerything. We eat at a table at a given time or times, we take a shower in the bathroom or at the well, we sleep in our room or the hallway of our home, or perhaps even outside, and we play soccer in the field when there is light. Likewise, it is desirable to get into the habit of doing meditation at the same time, same place. This is so that the mindbody does not have to deal with another variable when it is trying to be mindful of the mind.

This does not mean that meditation is what you do only at that given place or time. Meditation in the sense of mindfulness is something you do every waking minute of your life. Practicing religionists, Christian or other, would understand this well. Whether you are listening to me, or returning to your room or eating, or talking to someone on the phone or peeling a yam or a carrot at home or cooking or washing the dishes or sitting in church, you can practice mindfulness by simply being aware of what you are doing at a given moment in time.

5.1.3 "Subham": The concept of Wholeness in Pastoral Counselling in The Hindu Cultural Context

Padmasani J. Gallup[3]

is professor at the Madras Christian College and teaches Social Ethics

Confronted culture

Contemporary Indian culture reflects its millenia-old Hindu religious history. It continues to be characterised by caste hierarchy, subservience to authority, insularity and resistance to change, and ritualism, among other factors. Indian society has been challenged to change, confronted by a system of public education brought by Western trading powers and offered to all, by the process of modernization consequent to rapid adaption of Western science and technology, and by the awakening of hitherto oppressed and suppressed members within that society. Western formal education introduced into the Hindu socio-religious context with explosive ideas and ideology. Based on Christian conceptions of personhood and on convictions about the equality and preciousness of each individual, it faced a belief-system in which persons were ordered in a vertical, high-low, hierarchy in which all human effort was to be expended in the pursuit of *moksa* for the male members – the union of the human soul *(atman)* with the all-pervading *Brahman*. Straightaway this education was a challenge to traditional acceptance of inequality and called persons to corporate responsibility.

---

[3] Padmasani J. Gallup, in: Otto Stange, Pastoral Care & Context, Amsterdam 1992

One of the outcomes of this confrontation can be perceived in the psychosocial problems of everyday living faced by a number of persons. In order to identify issues for contextual counselling, we may begin with a brief outline of the Hindu view of the person, proceed to look at three recent incidents and their possible resolution, and examine the Hindu understanding of the goals of human endeavour for some clues to the search of wholeness.

Hindu view of the person

Hinduism, the religion of eightyfive percent of India's people, is non-credal: anyone can be a Hindu. As a religion, it is a way of life following certain laws, practices and rituals based on a hierarchical social structure. Purpose and meaning in life is to be found in the journey toward *moksa* of the *atman* of the male Hindu. This journey may take a number of rebirths. Souls of women may attain *moksa* as they are reborn as males. The laws governing individual and social life are set out in the *dharma* for each; a dharma is variously interpreted as "moral duty", "law" or "right action".

Over the centuries these laws have taken on a conserving rigidity which is almost impossible to change. Each person's *dharma* is proscribed within its limits of *desa* (country: cultural setting), *kala* (past and present history of cultural setting), *shrama* (the particular stage of life within the cycle of births) and *guna* (genetic, psycho-biological make-up).

The individual male is expected to develop along certain set ideals toward the ultimate goal. These ideas are articulated as psychological *ashramadharma* stages of life. Childhood is not recognized as a formal stage.

A not untypical modern, adult, Indian male

Kumar, a forty-plus government employee has a wife, Kala, a daughter, Jaya, aged seven, and a three year old son, Vimal – apparently an ideal, attractive Christian family. But, Kala, a competent college lecturer, poured out a narrative of acts of mental and physical violence perpetrated on her and the children by Kumar

126

over a span of years. Typically, Kumar would return home very late at night, having enjoyed an evening with friends or at a movie. He would wake the sleeping children because he "wanted to enjoy talking with them". Kala would have to prepare a fresh, hot dinner and wait on him while he ate. He never told her where he had been or what he had done. When he was full and sleepy, he would retire to bed regardless of the wakefullness of the others. He did not comprehend that there was anything amiss in his pattern of behaviour. These were the least offensive of his actions. He had no hesitation about beating and abusing his wife and children. Kala had had enough, and wondered what her options for a safe and quiet life would be.

The problem of Kumar may be identified as that of one who had not resolved the unconscious feelings of anger toward his mother. The mother happens to be another "typical case". She exerted such a pathological control over Kumar, her first-born, that she used to brush his teeth for him up to age eleven! The issue seems to be the complex one of the so-called "passive" Indian women safeguarding her own fragile ego by manipulating the male under her control. Her husband, inordinately proud of his son, indulged him to the extent that he never had a want, nor, one would suspect, any freedom to grow to be himself. Without freedom, he had not learned any responsibility, either. He took what he wanted, expected those around him to serve him, was filled with unrecognized rage against his mother, and took it out on his wife.

Search for wholeness in the mutuality of partnership – woman's status in Hindu culture

Hindu culture has allowed only a dependent identity for women. Some women live in relative peace and contentment, accepting and adjusting to this role. Those who have been absorbed in finding and providing the basic necessities for bringing up a family have developed the ego-strength of the survivor. Middle-class, eduated and economically independent women have faced the need for a concsciously independent identity for themselves and have of-

127

ten developed into stable adult personalities. Those who have not managed to appropriate independent identities adopt pathological strategies of control, especially of their sons. It is painfully true to those wives whose husbands act out their acknowledged rage against their mothers by abusing their wives. A vicious spiral results, of seeking identity through overt or covert control over those seen as weak or lesser beings (e.g., servants). However, Kala is attempting to break this spiral and is anxious to relate "normally" to her husband and children. The origin of the pathological relationship may be traced to the adult male. The expectation that all others are to serve the ultimate goal of the Hindu male legitimizes his use of others for the fulfillment of his wishes and desires. This can reach pathological dimensions of self-centredness and cause severe problems in relationships within a family. In joint family situations, the status of the grandfather is that of either a benevolent or tyrannical patriarch. Grown sons have to take on servient attitudes. The evolution of a pecking order in order to assume an identity is inevitable, with the attendant risk of hidden resentments.

Reinterpretation of the Hindu mythology

What is the task of pastoral counselling in the case of Kala? She could be encouraged to look at mythological heroines who undertake the task of bringing about change in situations of conflict. Indian mythology narrates stories about women who merge with strong identities in spite of all manner of vicissitudes; Sita, Savitri and Kannagi are such heroines. Damayanthi is one such. Her husband, Nalan, whom she herself chose amon all the princes who had attended her *swayamvaram*[4], turns out to be a gambler with wanderlust. After even losing the clothes off his back, he leaves Damayanthi, taking half of her sari to cover his nakedness. She returns to her father's house, but cannot rest. She organizes a second *swayamvaram* and choses the same Nalan, because, without a husband she

---

[4] The ancient practice of allowing the daughter of a wealthy citizen to choose her husband through publicly garlanding him in the company of a number of suitors.

cannot have sons to earn *moksa* for her, which*is* her only salvation. Her *dharma* dictates this. But she, being stronger and the more mature, becomes the rescuer, saving Nalan from his own folly so that he, too, can fulfil his *dharma*. Likewise, Kala must work out her own salvation by not only serving Kumar, but also by helping him to change his unacceptable behaviour. Hindu culture, while giving a low status to woman, elevates her to the status of a goddess (a giver) in the family as wife and mother.

> A wife is half the man transcends,
> In value for all other friends.
> She every earthly blessing brings,
> And even redemption from her springs.
> In lovely homes, companions bright,
> These charming women give delight;
> Like fathers wise, in duty tried,
> To virtuous acts they prompt and guide.
> Whenever we suffer pain and grief
> Like mothers kind they bring belief.

Mahabharata[5]

> A Father excels ten upadhyayas (teachers) in glory,
> But a mother excels a thousand fathers.

Manu[6]

This status-augmentation can be utilized to strengthen Kala in counselling. Counselling may encourage Kala to try to win Kumar over through patience and thoughtful care to evoke a sense of responsibility and a desire to be a partner in life. She must be cautioned against perpetuating the vicious spiral, and helped to deal constructively with her frustrations. Pastoral counselling would stress the eqality of men and women in creation, the mutuality of giving and receiving of care and love; it would recall the need to be

---

5   Hindu epic poem of 1000 B.D.
6   Codifier of Hindu law of 2. Century A.D.

a "house-holder" loving and caring for the young and weak. Kumar cannot be left in lonely splendour, but through a saving partnership of respect, through verbal and non-verbal communication husband and wife have to seek their good through responsible parenthood, released from unrealistic expectations of themselves and of each other. Kala does not wish to leave her husband. A separated or divorced woman is as full of bitterness as a widow. She is blamed, ostracised and cursed. Counselling is directed toward achieving the ideal wholeness of male-female partnership as visioned in the *Arthanareesvara* union of Siva and Parvathi, God of Hindu Sivaism. It is sometimes referred to as the union of Sivam and Sakti – goodness and power. In this search for wholeness the whole family, aunts, uncles, cousins etc. could be involved.

A college student: youth or adult

A young college junior was elected to the office of secretary of the students' union.

Straightaway he went to the women's hostel and announced that he would lead a strike as soon as the new academic year commenced. He saw no need to identify an issue for such "direct action".

Such a bid for a revolt can be recognised as a pathetic cry for recognition or notice. It can be seen as a part of the ultimate search for identity, and an acceptable world-view.

For a number of college-students the transition from a rural, simple, basic styled life to urban sophistication is discomforting if not shattering. From identity as a youngster dependent on parents and other elders in the village family, he is thrust willy-nilly into the role of budding expert or authority on world affairs, politics, economics, the sciences and technology. He is often forced into a position of responsibility and decision-making for which his psychological development has not prepared him. Even if he hails from an urban, middle-class family, sometimes this same situation obtains, especially if he is the first to attain university education. Relating to women becomes a behavioural issue in a co-educational institution for those brought up on strict taboos. Some rural and urban families do not allow brothers and sisters to have any normal sibling relationship after puberty. Some cannot even converse. The adolescent's awakening sexuality is rudely and pathologically suppressed and seeks outlets in unacceptable ways. The cultural ideal being abstinent or sex controlled towards procreation, there is much guilt. Masturbation and seminal emission are still believed to cause psychiatric disorders. This causes a split in value-orientation; the ideal being so far removed from experience.

Education in today's India becomes a factor in the confusion of youth. While rural or urban middle class ethos and social norms are founded on the stringent hierarchy of caste division, a student in the university is challenged to adopt consciously a life-style and attitude of equality. While his family assures him a status and position due to birth alone, away from his family he is told that he has to earn his status through hard work. In the dormitory a brahmin may well share sleeping quarters, dining and toilet facilities with an "untouchable". This may give rise to identity and role confusion. Role refusals result when freedom is pursued without its concomitant of responsibility in a situation where the youngster cannot identify "responsible living". He is also bombarded by differing and seductive ideologies. He may give in to fatalism.

Hindu cultural ethos, hoewever, engenders a mind set which manages to assume normal functioning in spite of contradictions. Compartmentalization is a coping mechanism adopted by the Indian psyche. Moreover, as Sudhir Kakar has identified, the primary process of thinking prevails among the young as well as adults, allowing the mind to hold contradictions together without causing psychic disorientation.

Search for holistic world view and viable identity

It is fairly well recognized that the Indian bio-social structure has not recognized adolescence as a developmental stage. Rites of passage observed formally, and sometimes without pomp and ceremony, at puberty for both boys and girls, mark the end of childhood and entrance into the adult world of work and responsibility. Both boys and girls had been indulged and surrounded with warmth and affection as children. Now the young boy is required to take his place with the men, in the fields and elsewhere and be gainfully employed. The young girl leaves innocent playfullness, joins the women in their subservient functions, is constrained to guard her chastity most vigilantly, and becomes a caregiver. There is neither the leisure nor the stimulus to begin to reflect about "Who am I?" or "What am I?" Most youngsters accept an imposed identity. Perhaps this is why the Hindu adult male seems constrained to devote energy and time in an attempt at self-realization in late adulthood and old age.

In psychosocial development in Western cultures, adolescence is a distinct stage during which the search for an identity predominates. The crisis of this stage, according to Erikson, is "identity" versus "identity confusion" and the virtue is "fidelity"[7].

Sudhi Kakar relates this stage and the preceding one of school age to the two parts of the first *ashramadharma*, that of Brahmacharya:

" … in which the school child, growing into youth, learned the basic skills relevant to his future adult working role, while he lived together with other students and the guru.The task I would say, lies in the knowing of one's dharma, which could consist of acquiring the skills in one's caste and in winning identity based on a caste identity and the identification with and emulation of the guru."[8]

This is an ancient ideal. In today's world it is not possible. While a young student may manage to hold together the contradictions of a casteless campus life-style and Hindu family ethos of strict caste oberservance, he/she still has to know who she/he is.

An equally serious issue is a viable world-view to which the youngster can be committed. The Hindu world-view is necessarily crumbling as India gets catapulted into a world capitalist economy from a rural-based barter system, and into a techno-dominated

[7]   Erik H. Erikson: Childhood and Identity
[8]   Kakar, Sudhir, ed.: Identity and Adulthood, p. 7

world. India is rapidly being sucked into the global village. Its youth is challenged to make meaningful life in this globale village where nuclear warheads have been stockpiled with the potential of blowing up the whole planet earth; where neutron bombs will spare the Taj Mahal but will not leave any living being to enjoy it; where bomb-making has been made as simple, and maybe as satisfying, as assembling a tinker-toy structure for an elementary school-child. Modernization and dependance on technology has given rise to a sense of helplessness or powerlessness and man becomes less important than machine.

Consequently, young persons in colleges are confused and cynical. There is no "identification with and emulation of the Guru". Their professors do not practice what they profess. Yet, the youngsters do hunger for a *guru-sishya* (master-disciple) relationship; they want ideals and seek for leaders with power and charisma. The only power they encounter may be that of violence and terror; there is no grace. Or they get sucked into fatalism.

Counselling in this context for confused, leaderless young persons may have to adopt the directive approach of the rational-emotive type. Leading the youngsters to search in their superego, they may find a residue of the moral and ethical teachings of the ancients. They can be encouraged to examine their own literature to recapture the idealism and ethical norms of a viable world view (e.g. the couplets of the *Tirukkural*, on right daily living based on charity, love and peace).

Venkoba Rao suggests the use of the *Bhagavadgita*, which offers "the concept of total surrender, eagerness of the pupil to enlighten himself, liberty to interrogate intelligently, desire for knowledge to dispel ignorance, and absence of coercion on the part of the counsellor.[9] The disciplines of Yoga may be introduced at this stage so that students may freely choose the path most suited to them. While encouraging the young persons to pursue freedom at this stage, they should be helped to accept responsibility as the other side of the coin. They soon shall acquire the *ashrama* of householder and care-

---

[9] Rao, in: Transcultural Psychiatry, John J. Cox, Ed., p. 302

giver, and must be prepared.

There can be a viable identity as a human, and Indian, without the constrictions of casteism and communalism. The human is to be understood in the wholeness of body, mind and spirit without the guilt associated with sexuality. The Christian acceptance of human beings as created in God's image includes physiological, psychological and spiritual entities. To assist the youngsters to accept this and work toward such an identity is the task of pastoral counselling. Search for wholeness will be integrating self-identity with a viable world-view. At this age young women and men are keen on ecological concerns. The Indian view of the spark of the divine in each created being could help in articulating environmental concerns and corporate responsibility.

India's contribution to the search of wholeness

Perhaps a significant contribution of Indian culture is that it takes religion seriously. Every aspect of life, every prescribed duty, is learned within the framework of Hindu religion. The most greedy entrepreneur, the most corrupt politician, will begin his day with *puja* (worship) at the household shrine (or his wife does it on his behalf). Being in touch, however remotely, with the source of Being keeps the heart and mind on an even keel. Guilt is not a burden as heavy experienced as in Christendom, because the Hindu system acknowledges repeated chance through the cycle of births for working out one's *dharma*, for making amends and for atonement.

The negative aspect of this religious foundation for all life's rituals is that it becomes forced and unnatural, even inhuman. This is why Mahatma Gandhi, a staunch Hindu, accepted the teachings of Jesus as possessing universal applicability, and the stalwarts who hammered out the constitution for the socialist republic of India insisted that it be strictly secular while adopting a number of principles from the Biblically-influenced constitution of the United Stated of America.

Exercises such as meditation and the different systems of Yoga are meant at enable the individual to attain adult maturity. Concepts of adulthood are integral to the Hindu world view, which seeks to give meaning to life. Since the world image focuses on liberation of the *atman*, two stages of adulthood are posited: one to fulfill all the *dharma* of living in the world with others in a variety of relationships; the next: a conscious withdrawal from all worldly attachments and preparation for the ultimate union with Brahman in death. As Kakar observes, the healthy adult of western understandings (derived from psychoanalysis of pathological persons), is "only a prelude to the liberated adult. Ideally adulthood does not stop at prudence, but must lead towards liberation."

Hindu culture and philosophy has assumed that there is a higher order of knowledge (*vidhya*), available to humans which will lead them to liberation beyond nature and radically different from physical, sensory knowledge (*avidhya*). It has evolved four systems of Yoga as disciplines which will lead to this *vidhya* and consequent liberation.

Karma does not require physical withdrawal, but enjoins activity which is disinterested and detached; activity according to the *ashrama* of the householder for the care of others.

Bakhti Yoga is the path of pure devotion leading to the spirituality of total dependence on the godhead and forgetfulness of the physical self.

Gnana Yoga furnishes knowledge through intellectual exercise of meditation and mental practices.

Raja Yoga utilizes psycho-physiological techniques to transform the habitual modes of experiencing. Through intense concentration a feeling of oneness with the objects of creation is achieved as well as a hereto unknown intensity of awareness.

All of these paths lead to the detachment necessary for leaving this earthly life gracefully, in a realistic and natural aceptance of the inevitable. They may also take the individual beyond this initial purpose to an "exaltation" beyond all human imaginings, to the *samadhi* and *santhi* of total union in *moksa*. *Santhi* is a concept of wholeness, of full integration of mind, body and spirit offered through the yogic systems of hard discipline that Hindu culture can offer for all persons. The whole yogic journey can be interpreted as the way that the self escapes isolation and the finality of death through identification on a grand, universal scale, with the universe of matter and spirit.

Contextual counselling in India aims toward adult maturity and takes seriously the Hindu world view, expectations, goals and liberative principals, adapting, countering, and working through them in response to individual needs.

Pastoral counselling brings in the Christian concern for the wholeness, the blessed well-being of all persons. It would seek to counteract the fatalism and indifference, which arises out of the Hindu world view, toward human suffering and the powers of evil. At the same time it would search for aspects that would help to bring wholeness in the Hindu culture.

Much of this paper is conceptual. The case of Kala is the one in process now. It is hoped that counsellors in India could try these concepts and evolve others to bring wholeness to suffering and hurting persons. It is also hoped that the place of the faith community in this endeavour and search for wholeness in pastoral counselling would be explored by others. We Indians are community oriented, not individualist as Western people tend to be. Cross-cultural counselling could use community as an agent for bringing wholeness, the *subham* of blessedness.

5.1.4   Native Stories for Transition in a Strange Land

Edna Manitowabi[10]

then is professor of Native Studies at Trent University in Peterborough/Canada. She is an Elder of the Ishnobi from Manitoulin Island in Northern Ontario

Good Morning: In my language, bonjour and it's not bon jour, it's bonjour – in my language, Ojibway, that's the nation I'm from and that is my first language.

---

[10]   A lecture delivered in Toronto/Canada, 1995, in: James Reed: Babylon and Jersualem. Stories for Transition in a Strange Land

Just a brief introduction about myself that will tell you where I am coming from and my walk, where it has brought me and from where I have emerged. It' s not only the fact that I was born and raised on Manitoulin Island of Ojibway-Odaway parents and sent to a residential school at a very early age in my life, my childhood took me to a place in my 20's where I began to wander and wonder, wonder about life, the sacredness of life. I came to a place in my life where I felt that I was only existing but not really being. I came to a place where I was lost with no sense of identity, no sense of who I am, who I was. I was trying to fit in a white man's world. I was trying to be white and somewhere deep down with me, in my soul, I knew that I could never be white no matter how hard I tried to move and act in that way, even when I dyed my hair blonde. There was *that* until I came to a place where there was only darkness; there was no direction.

Dreams have always been very important to our people, my people, and it was at that time, in my darkness, that I had a dream experience. For us dreams are mentors, our teachers, and so there was that which I would call the awakening for me, the awakening of spirit, spirit trying to communicate with me. And that there was more to life than just existing. In this dream I was taken to a place, a spiritual place, a beautiful, beautiful place where I felt an incredible love, a joy. Those are nice words and the experience, the vision that I saw was just so huge, so beautiful, it filled me with a great love, a great joy.

And from the dream experience I was able to come back. But, at first I didn't want to because I felt that there was nothing here for me. I couldn't see. Like I said, there was no direction. In this dream experience I finally did because there was a voice that called out to me: "Come back. You have to come back". When I came back I started to think about that experience, and when I felt that love there was a sense of wanting to find out who I am. Who am I? Where am I going? Where did I come from? What is my purpose? Those four things were very strong for me.

Who am I? It wasn't enough to say I am Edna Manitowabi. I was born and raised on Manitoulin Island. I was born of Ojibway Odaway parents. That wasn't enough. I need to find who I am. Who I am and I need to know where I was going. But in order to know where you are going, in order to be able to see where one is going, you need to be able to know where you came from. That was strong. Where did I come from beyond my home, my reservation, my community, my parents, my family? Roots seem to stand out – tradition, culture, language, music, stories, our myths, our legends, creation stories, our ceremonies, our rituals. That's what I felt very strong. So from that point I began to search, research, to try and recover and discover what was in our history, retracing steps, looking for grandmothers and grandfathers. Who should talk to me? Who would talk to me about identity, about those things that were lost and scattered along the way? Because that's what happened. The other one is purpose. What is my purpose? I realized from that dream experience that we all come into the world for a purpose, for a reason. We all grind gifts, beautiful gifts, every one of us is a beautiful spirit that comes to experience this beautiful journey.

And so began my spiritual journey in my late 20s, a hunger and a thirst to find who I am, my identity, my culture because those things on our history were banned and outlawed because they were not understood. They were seen as big pagan, heathen. But for an Ishnobi, for the aboriginal people, the indigenous people of this Turtle Island, they had a very, very deep respect for our mother the earth, for this creation. They saw that all of creation we were a part of that and they are our relatives. We don't worship them, but we are related to them and we know that there is an interconnectedness to all things, a part of this beautiful, beautiful creation, the mother Earth, the grandmothers and grandfathers in the four sacred directions. So when I first started I didn't have a direction and I went and sought out my grandmothers. In them were the stories of our ancestors. It's in their blood memory; it's in their genes. They had not forgotten even though five hundred years of oppression, of genocide, of a culturation tried to suppress.

That's my introduction. And so began my journey because when I looked around in my community, our reservations I saw a lot of pain, a lot of suffering, sorrow, grieving, grieving the past, grieving, mourning what has been lost since Europeans, since the light-skinned race came on to our shores. They brought with them a different kind of concept. They brought with them a different kind of thinking, a different way of seeing, the concept of ownership. Whereas with us it was to share, divide and conquer, with us and with our people. There was a special relationship with all of creation and that we saw each other being a part, as brothers and sisters equal. There was that and that we needed each other in order to survive, in order to live on Mother Earth, in order to live on this creation.

Sometimes ago I went about visiting with my grandmothers and my grandfathers across this country, looking for those things that have been lost, there was a great sense that my people needed to heal. When I was going through the Residential School Syndrome and all those things that got along with that – the sexual abuse, the loss of what we have lost – I wanted to find something that would help our people and I thought the old ones would have an answer, would help. And because so many of our people turned our backs from our grandmothers and our grandfathers and took up a different way, a foreign way, a way that was different, a way that originally didn't belong to us, they hesitated and they weren't sure. But when they saw that I was wanting desperately to heal, they began to share their stories and their telling their stories. I began to feel. For the first time in my life I began to feel as though I am alive. I have life, there is life within me. And they nurtured that, they fed that. Their stories, their teachings, their songs, their music nurtured my spirit and helped me to come back to life, to feel life again, feel that life is worth living. And all the years of my going to psychiatrists, psychologists, social workers, that kind of counselling, that kind of helping didn't help me because I wasn't seen as a human being. I wasn't seen as a person. Instead I was seen as a number, a client; but those grandmothers – they saw me as a child, a very, very precious child, a beautiful child, and they allowed me to sit with them and to listen. I couldn't sleep because I was so hungry; I was thirsty for that knowledge. And so I began to grow and evolve spiritually, I wanted that for my people and so I came home. It was the Cree people that got me started, and they did say even though we may be aboriginal people to this Turtle Island we have many different nations and we have our own languages, our own way of viewing the world. There is that and there is that respect. We still see each other as related, as brothers and sisters, being a part of Mother Earth.

I want to share this prophecy with you. It talks about two faces, two people. It talks about peace and brotherhood. It talks about where we have been, our hope for the future, our vision, our goals and our aspirations. They talk about this time as being the time of the Seventh Fire. There were prophets that came amongst our people and there was a prophecy that was given way before the light-skinned race came, even maybe before they even thought about it. This prophet said there is a light-skinned race that is coming. Be careful! We don't know yet what face he is going to come wearing. He will either come wearing one of two faces – the face of destruction or the face of brotherhood. If he comes wearing the face of brotherhood, not to worry because he will welcome him as brother, and we will live together in peace and harmony. But if he doesn't come wearing that face of brotherood and comes wearing the face of destruction, then, my children, you will experience a great destruction that you have never experienced before. And so we know, we know because of what we have been through the past five hundred years what kind of face that he came wearing. He didn't come wearing the face of brotherhood. He came wearing the face of destruction. We have seen *that* the past five hundred years, since the time of contact and how our people are still today, in our communities, we still see, we still see that, what they are feeling. It's like we have been through a great storm, an incredible storm, that we have been in the eye of the storm the past five hundred years.

Two things have to happen. In the time of the Seventh Fire, our people, the Ishnobi, the different first nations people of this fertile island must be able to pick up those things that have been lost and scattered along the way and that's why I have become a very strong advocate of traditions and culture, the sacredness, those things that say who we are as a people, our language. Our language says who we are. Our spirit, our soul says who we are and it is the expression, we express that through our culture, through our dances, our music, our songs, those things have been banned and outlawed. It's only within the last fifty years that the sundance, within the last twenty years we were able to practise our ceremonies. When you take that spirituality from a people something happens; when our children were away from our communities. Children are the most precious beings; they are our heart, so just imagine what happened to a whole community of people when the priests, the nuns, the churches came and took those children from those communities. They committed a great wrong. It's like you tear the heart out of a mother when you take the child and place that child in a foreign environment at a very early age. When a child at a very early age is being moulded and shaped by the ones that love him, that care about her. That didn't happen for us. We became robots. We became conditions to move, to behave, to think in a different way. That's what happened to me. That's why the attempted suicides; that's why (there is) loss.

Today there is an incredible renaissance that is happening. It started in the 60s. And I'm one of those that found that connection with tradition, culture and spirituality; those things that connect me to my true mother. We have an umbilical bond. There is that connection with the Earth, a very, very strong connection and I wanted to find out who am I. An Ishnobi? And a grandmother said to me if you want to find out who you are then go and sit with your mother, your real mother. I did that. I sat with her. I talked to the trees. I talked to the birds. I talked to the four legends, the simmers, the crawlers, all of these things that grow and I began to see how much I am part of all that. I am a woman. I am sacred and holy.

There's another concept that was brought here that was different. For us, as aboriginal people, a woman was always held with great honour and respect because of the way she is, the way she is the creator; she is the one that brings forth life. She is the one doorway in which life can come into the world. We were not taken from somebody's rib, but that's the story that was brainwashed to us. But in our teachings we are told woman is sacred. She is doubly blessed and one of her blessings is the fact that she is the doorway, the only doorway in which spirit can come into this world. No other way. It's the woman who takes that child, the spirit, that life and molds and shapes that life inside of her. What she thinks, what she eats, goes into nourishing and feeding that life moulding and shaping her thoughts. She's creating that life. She's responsible for that water, she was given that great blessing to look after that water just like our grandmother moon, our mentor, our teacher. We have special relationships with the moon. She is the one who looks after, regulates those cycles, the seasons, the tides. She has a responsibility. The sun, our brother, the sun has a responsibility, has a job to do. He still does it. He still comes and gives us light and warmth every day, and we greet that light, the creator's light. Balance in all of creation – there is that, the universal man, the universal woman. When that child is ready to issue forth that woman is the number one teacher, first teacher, unconditional love. She puts her child to her breast and even that we stop doing as mothers. Carnation was brought here – Carnation milk, cow's milk. Maybe that's why our children began to behave like cows. In putting her child to her breast, she was the first teacher, the first nurturer and in that way she was teaching and showing kindness. She was sharing of herself, she was giving up herself, taking that time to be with that life, to nurture, to give life, to teach, and giving strength. Woman was given a helper to do that work, to do that creation. And we refer to man as?, helps and looks after this creation. He's a helper. He's not one to take control and dominate, and he's a helper, helper of Mother Earth, helper of woman. That were our original instructions, but what happened? Something was brought here, a different way of thinking was brought here. The time of contact, what was happening over there, across that big body of water. They were killing their women. Patriarchy. They had lost a connection to their true mother, their real mother, the Earth. I heard one of my grandfathers, he's one that I refer to as a high priest, Old One from the Mountains, he said: "You know they referred to this country as the new country, the new world, and over there they refer to it as the old world, old country." He says: "you know over there they make her old. They made her old over there where there are places now she can't give. She's tired and that's why they came over here to this new and beautiful where she is still young and beautiful. But I wonder for how long? That's up to us. That's up to you. Are we going to keep her young and beautiful or are we going to desecrate her like woman has been desecrated? Woman, the creator, the lifegiver has been raped, has been degraded. Women is like the Earth. What happens to one happens to the other and maybe those of us who are female, who are woman and Ishnobi will stand up and speak for our mother, the Earth. Enough is enough. We need to take care of our mother the Earth. We need to help her stay young and beautiful. There are places where she is so incredibly beautiful and times of sorrow, of grief, of sadness. I have gone to those places and sat and received her healing, her nourishment, her soothing, her embrace, and I'm able to get up and get on with life.

Those are some of the things that have to happen in the time of the Seventh Fire. Our people have to pick up those things to feel good about who we are – self-esteem, self-confidence, self-worth – because that is something that was stripped from them, and we are just now trying to pick up those things, to feel good about who we are. I have begun ways to help youth and one of them is through the university – Native Studies. One of the ways is through theatre; theatre is a great medicine. It heals that body, mind and spirit and that way our youth, our young people are beginning to find their voices, their music, their songs, and in finding their music and their songs their stories. They are healing. There has to be that. We have to heal and that's where we are at this time, the time of healing, an incredible, beautiful time where there is a sense of coming to life. It's like we have been robots for a long, long time, and now an Ishnobi is standing up. Eli Harper, when he said "No", one word that's what it represented for us. No more. No more abuse. No more desecration. Get off my toes so I can stand up and do for myself. Stop standing on my feet. Stop holding me back. Stop treating me as though I can't do for myself. I am not your child – and there has been that mentality. The churches have come and treated us in that way, children who can't look after themselves. The Great White Father is going to do that for you, that's the patriarchy. A lot of us are going back to our mother the Earth to be given that responsibility to do it for ourselves. I'm not saying that we don't need your help. What I am saying is we need to see each as brothers and sisters, as family. We are all a part of his creation, this Mother Earth. No matter what colour we are, not matter what religion, what denomination: spirituality is not an institution. It's not a religion, it's not an organization. Spirituality has to do with the heart and that's the way that I have tried to speak this morning, from the heart. Not as an academic, but from the heart, from my experience, from where I have been. What my hopes and my aspirations are and my hope and my prayer is at all people, not matter where we come from, no matter what language, no matter what our beliefs. That we will see each other as human beings and treat each other as human beings with feelings, with emotions. I have a heart, I have feelings and that we all come from the same mother. That's one thing that we have in common.

We all need the earth in order to survive. So how we are going to do that? How are we going to help her? We have to recognize our differences and that one people is not better than the other, that we are all related, that we have one mother, we are her children and to have that personal relationship with her. Don't be shy. Don't be afraid. Don't be timid to have that relationship, a personal relationship with the Earth. Touch her. Touch that tree. When you hear a bird singing, what is that bird saying? Let it touch your heart. Allow nature to soothe you, to communicate with you because there is that and it's great and beautiful prayer. She is my source. That's where I go for healing. I go for my mother. I go and tell her where I have been. So in the time of the Seventh Fire those ones in the time of contact who came wearing the face of destruction when they were supposed to be wearing the face of brotherhood, at this time they have that responsibility to put on that face of brotherhood now and our people, my people have a responsibility to pick up. We all have a responsibility, every one of us to help one another, to care for one another, not to help in a way that you're saying that you're better or I'm going to do it for you where it's disempowering but to help in a way that empowers people. They are able to do for themselves, to take control of their own destinies and that's what we want to do at this time. We are doing. The time of the Seventh Fire is a beautiful time of great changes, of evolution and there is the promise of the Eigth Fire when all people will be a part of that fire, all races, all colours, all religions will see that we are all related, that we are all brothers and sisters. The Eigth Fire promises peace and brotherhood and sisterhood of all nations and people and that's what I work towards. That's what I work for. I have many students come to Native studies of different nations and that's where I teach from, that's where I share from, that's the way that I teach, that we come together as brothers and sisters making bridges, healing bridges. It's a healing time. It's a time of reconciliations, it's a time of resolving. So the Seventh Fire talks about that face of brotherhood, sisterhood and that my people will pick up those tools. They won't be jailed for it, whereas in the past they have been.

I would like to finish with a song, if I may. This song talks about, it's a prophecy song and what it says, is:

"Get up now. Wake up. Wake up. And when I hear that wake up, it's like my spirit is being told to wake up. Open yourself, open that doorway whether you want to see it as your spiritual eye or that soft spot so that open your ears and hear creation, hear your mother, what she has to say. Hear the grandmothers, the grandfathers, what they have to say to you. Open your heart and it's the way that we move that's how we will be recognized, the way that we sound, our actions".

That's the prophecy song and it's like a prayer. It is a prayer that talks about the way that we are, the way that we move. That's how we will be seen by this creation, treating each other, in the four directions. Treat each other in a good and sacred manner. That's how treaties are made. There was an unwritten law. We all treat each other in a good and sacred way. We will honour each other. We will respect what has been done here.

Those are the blessing, the original instructions, the four directions: kindness, sharing, honesty and strength. We have a symbol here and the symbol that we use is sweetgrass, a braid of sweetgrass. The sweetgrass symbolized the hair of our Mother, the Earth, and so when you got to some native communities you will see some old women and old men with their hair braided and that talks about themselves, body, mind and spirit. And it talks about that connection with the Earth, with creation. The sweetgrass, it's braided in three – body, mind and spirit but also like this eagle feather. Kindness, sharing, honesty, that's what makes us strong. Using those principles, those gifts, and wearing it. When I first went to those grandmothers and grandfathers, that's the way they talked to me. Wear it, put it on. The difference between white values and native values is how we use those, how we wear them. The other one is sharing and the symbol that we use for that one is the animal, the four-leggeds, the swimmers, the crawlers, the fiers because they are the ones in order to survive we ask them for their lives. In order to feed our loved ones, to put food on the table, they gave up their lives and that's the highest form of sharing. So that we might have life. Sharing. Honesty is that tree, tree of life. The tree stands straight, to live in an honest way, to be honest with the creator, to be honest with your mother, with all your relatives, the four directions. And the roots, the roots go into the Earth, they're rooted to the ground, the Earth where the tree is being nourished and nurtured by the Earth again, the Mother. The branches go out and this talks about we see your life there, our life, my life. When I look at a tree, I see my life. The branches, the mini branches, the mini paths that we go off to find, to search, to heal, looking. Mini teachings, mini learning, and in our workshops we will be talking about that – the Seven Stages of Life.

I don't know if I have talked about healing here and counselling, but I do know that it's my way and it's the way that I have learned. It's the way that I have been healed, and I have gathered growth and knowledge. It's the way that I have talked about it – through the songs, through the stories, my Mother, the Earth, my relatives, creation. The beauty of my language, the culture, that we have something really beautiful, and I'm so rich. I don't have great material things, but I am rich. I am very rich. I have been blessed with beautiful, beautiful children. I have grandchildren, and they have changed my life, my grandchildren. I see them as great blessings, spirits that come into the world. In a time of great darkness my granddaughter was born and brought me to life, brought me light, helped me to see. So I wanted to finish with that prayer.

5.1.5 Spirituality and counselling for healing and liberation: The context and praxis of African pastoral activity and psychotherapy

Jean Masamba ma Mpolo[11]

then is professor at the Protestant Faculty of Kinshasa, Zaire

My original intention was to write on counselling for liberation. However, due to the fact that counselling is rooted in the socio-cultural, philosophical, political and religious contexts of the people for which it is practiced. I thought it appropriate to share some ideas on what seems to be patterns by which traditional and most africans view and experience healing and deliverance as a spiritual and counselling process for wholeness and liberation.

Healing only by the use of the spiritual dimension such as prayer is one of the new phenomena attracting thousands of people to the Christian churches in Africa today. It seems to be the quickest and easiest methodological approach to counselling for liberation from anxiety, fear, attack from evil spirits and as a way to seek protection from socio-economic and possible political aggression. Counselling solely through the spiritual healing approach is, however, contrary to the traditional ways of looking at life and methods of organising therapy for the healing and liberation of individuals and communities.

Traditional African cultures organised their thoughts and health systems in ways which did not relegate healing to the sole realm of the spiritual. Thus, the economics and politics of "spiritual healing" are an issue of great concern. Africa is invaded by spiritualities often untouched by the deep need of the poor. We are faced with a

---

[11] This article was first published in: The Church and Healing. Echoes from Africa, p. 11-35. There are presented extracts from original texts.

dualistic spirituality, a self-satisfying individualistic pietism which reinforces the economic exploitation and political domination of the poor.

Pietism, whether personal or corporate, is often chosen over against the social implications of the Gospel. Some of us in Africa interested in pastoral care and counselling and related pastoral studies are less preoccupied with the development of methods intending for spiritual healing, that is, techniques which dwell on healing only through religion.

Rather we are looking at healing in the wider context of African spirituality which incorporates all dimensions of human and cosmic life. Healing through prayer alone would impoverish the pastoral ministry and the witness of the Church in Africa and isolate it from the mainstream of forces that should contribute to the development and liberation of the African people.

It is almost a cliché to say that the African sees life as one integral whole. Every profession and event has its spiritual dimension. Though distinguishable from one another politics, economics, ethics, ecology, marriage and family life are inseparable from one another, and each was an integral part of religion. This makes Bishop Peter Sarpong of Ghana to say:

"To the African, religion is like the skin that you carry along with you wherever you are, not like the cloth that you wear now and discard the next moment."

This makes most people seek solutions to their various problems in terms of their traditional spirituality. Christian Baeta[12] makes the following observation:

'Traditionally in Ghana, the solution to all problems of ill-health, as of concern or anxiety generally has been sought squarely within the framework of religion. On a world-view which assumes the effective presence of numberless spirits and regards all life as one; with no clear distinctions between the material and the non-material, the natural and the supernat-

---

[12] Christian Baeta is a theologian living and working in Ghana

ural let alone the secular and religious; or even between man and other things and beings, this could hardly be otherwise.'[13]

We are aware of the many forces that altered traditional spirituality. Assaulted by Western and Arab political, cultural, educational and religious domination, the African people have experienced some changes in their personal and communal identities as well as in the ways they look at the world.

The fact is, however, that the persistence of the traditional African spirituality is an observable factor that has been documented by many researchers. Thus, neither colonization, christianization or the slave enterprise has completely eradicated the traditional African spirituality and world-view in the Black continent as well as in South America, the Carribean and North America where Black Africans were taken as slaves.

Similar folk religions, typical Black Christian Worship experiences, funeral practices, health systems and family organizations found in Black communities around the world, give testimony to the existence and the persisting nature of Black spirituality.

In his study on African conversion, Horton notes that the African took from Islam and Christianity aspects of these new religions which met their needs; they maintained the relation between African religious belief, prophecy and healing against the wish of the historical Churches which had abandoned these aspects of spiritual activity.

Many Africans converted to Christianity run back to traditional spirituality especially when they have to find solutions to misfortune and poor health. People cling to African traditional spirituality as it contains positive human possibilities for wholeness and offers a kind of repository of other option beside Christian and western therapeutic and medical systems.

Christian missionary spirituality, especially in the nineteenth century, attributed great importance to personal piety and to the union of the soul with Jesus Christ. Piety was expressed through

---

[13] The citation is implied in Jean Masamba ma Mpolo's text, taken from: Baeta, C.G."Christianity and Healing"

rules and observances. This spirituality dwelt on denial and rejection of African traditional customs such as polygamy, communal living, belief in ancestral celebrations, and traditional therapies and medical systems. With some few exceptions, misssionary spirituality was characterized by varying degrees of intolerance and aggressiveness. Missionary dualistic Christianity exhalted the soul over against the body, opposed redemption to creation, the invisible to the visible, the sacred to the secular and the abstract to the concrete.

This spirituality was mainly concerned with the other world, with an emphasis on self-denial. The world was primarily looked at as a threat and as a source of contagion. It spiritualized even the doctrine of salvation. This is what Bosch, the American anthropologist, has said:

"Behind this lies the gnostic heresy that only the abstract, the idea, is the true being; the concrete physical, by contrast, is in reality non-being, illusion. This spiritualization reached its peak at the time when the entire biblical message was allegorized, when, for instance, a sermon on the miraculous healing of lepers was taken to refer only to the leprosy of sin from which we needed to be healed."(Bosch 1983:498).

Christian missionary spirituality ignored the cultural and psychic materials provided by traditional interpretation of dreams. The usual explanation given to the dreamers especially by confessors in the catholic parish mission is that the dreamer was not responsible for what was happening while sleeping, as in this state of mind, the human being was viewed as being entirely passive. As ancestors usually appeared in the dream materials, to take dreams seriously was seen as an offence to God who said: "You shall have no other gods against me" (Ex. 30,3). Ancestors were viewed as being the other gods. Dreams and visions characteristic of traditional African spirituality were seen as manifestations of hidden evil intentions of the "natives". This missionary attitude was in opposition to the Old and New Testament traditions in which, as in traditional African spirituality, dreams and visions are also considered as media of God's revelation.

Christian missionary spirituality ignored the universality of

God's revelation. From the beginning of creation God's spirit covered the while inhabited world (Gen.1,1-2), enabling also the African people to have communion with Him and to create their own social structures and systems of health, healing and liberation.

When examining the *Babalowo* medical systems among the *Yoruba*, the *Lemba* among the Kongo, and when one looks at the *Usenakpo*, a group of people specializing in the treatment of mentally disturbed patients in the *Igbo* society, or the *Ngangambuki*, the healing doctors and the elders of the clans presiding over reconciliation sessions in the Kongo society, one is amazed by the existence of complex theories and therapies in response to afflictions and all types of domination. At present, there exists a whole variety of religious traditions in Africa: Islam, mainline Protestantism, evangelical Protestantism, Liberal and Roman Catholicism, Anglicanism, Orthodox traditions, African traditional religion, etc. Each and all have an impact on present African spirituality. Africa is a continent and not a country. Its different ethnic groups have a variety of ways of looking at life and organizing health systems. But, even in the face of cultural change due to the influence of other religious traditions and western technology, certain elements are common and can be found in different forms in which Homo Africanus organized health systems, worship services and fought against domination and injustice.

5.2 Approaches

Ulrike Elsdörfer

Peace

Islam

"Since all religions are interested in the well-being of mankind this purpose is defeated if they cause conflict, injustice and violence. It is very saddening to a truly religious person to see people of the same religion attack each other".[14]

Responsibility

Islam

"Man has not come on planet earth by his own choice. He is here for a purpose. Only religion recognizes this fact and defines this purpose. It is to serve the creator. Serving God starts with the recognition and acknowledgement of the existence of God, caring for, and loving all creation. The purpose of religion is to provide peace. Peace among humans; peace between man and all living things; peace between man and his environment".[15]

Wholeness

Hinduism

"All of these paths lead to the detachment necessary for leaving this earthly life gracefully, in a realistic and natural acceptance of the inevitable. They may also take the individual beyond this initial purpose to an "exaltation" beyond all human imaginings, to the *samadhi* and *santhi* of total union in *moksa*. *Santhi* is a concept of wholeness, of full integration of mind, body and spirit offered through the yogic systems of hard discipline that Hindu culture can offer for all persons. The whole yogic journey can be interpreted as the way that the self escapes isolation and the finality of death through identification on a grand, universal scale, with the universe of matter and spirit."[16]

Awareness – Mindfulness

Buddhism

"This does not mean that meditation is what you do only at that given place or time. Meditation in the sense of mindfulness is something you

---

[14] Fuad Sahin: Islam Stories for Transition in a Strange Land,s. a.
[15] Fuad Sahin: Islam Stories for Transition in a Strange Land,s. a.
[16] Padmasani J. Gallup: "Subham": The Concept of Wholeness in Pastoral Counselling in The Hindu Cultural Context

do every waking minute of your life. Practicing religionists, Christian or other, would understand this well. Whether you are listening to me, or returning to your room or eating, or talking to someone on the phone or peeling a yam or a carrot at home or cooking or washing the dishes or sitting in church, you can practice mindfulness by simply being aware of what you are doing at a given moment in time."[17]

Sacredness – Liberation

Native religion

"I have begun ways to help youth and one of them is through the university – Native Studies. One of the ways is through theatre; theatre is a great medicine. It heals that body, mind and spirit and that way our youth, our young people are beginning to find their voices, their music, their songs and in finding their music and their songs and their stories. They are healing. We have to heal and that's where we are at this time, the time of healing, an incredible, beautiful time where there is a sense of coming to life. It's like we have been robots for a long, long time, and now an Ishnobi is standing up … "[18]

Spirituality

Native Religion

"We are all a part of his creation, this Mother Earth. No matter what colour we are, no matter what religion, what denomination: spirituality is not an institution. It's not a religion, it's not an organization. Spirituality has to do with the heart and that's the way that I have tried to speak this morning, from the heart."[19]

---

[17] Suwanda H. J. Sugunasiri: Buddhist Stories for Transition in a Strange Land
[18] Edna Manitowabi: Native Stories for Transition in a Strange Land
[19] Edna Manitowabi: Native Stories for Transition in a Strange Land

Ulrike Elsdörfer

Healing

Native Religion

"It's a healing time. It's a time of reconciliations, it's a time of resolving. So the Seventh Fire talks about that face of brotherhood, sisterhood and that my people will pick up those tools. They won't be jailed for it, whereas in the past they have been".[20]

---

[20] Edna Manitowabi: Native Stories for Transition in a Strange Land

Part III

6   Africa in pastoral care and counselling

The African Association for Pastoral Studies and Counselling came into being in February 1985, after an ecumenical meeting held in Limuru, Kenya, and was initiated by Professor Jean Masamba ma Mpolo from Zaire together with the World Council of Churches. At the same conference a series on pastoral care and counselling in Africa was founded, edited by Emmanuel Y. Lartey, Daisy Nwachuku, Kasonga wa Kasonga and Jean Masamba ma Mpolo. The texts introduced in this chapter are published in this series. Extracts are presented in the following chapter.

The following are the major aims of the AAPSC:

To promote and foster the advancement of pastoral studies and counselling from a distinctively African perspective.

To create a forum for the exchange of ideas and experience of pastoral concern in Africa and to help raise such issues to a focal point.

To promote and foster an awareness of the spiritual, psychological and social processes taking place in Africa as they relate to Pastoral Studies and Counselling and to consider their theological significance.

To stimulate greater understanding and co-operation among students of African Pastoral Studies and Counselling

To open up avenues and encourage specialized consultations, publications, training research, clinical education and supervision in pastoral studies relevant to the African situation.[1]

---

[1]   These aims are published in: W. Becher, A. Campbell, K. Parker: The Risks of Freedom, p. 21 / 22

6.1 Documents

With one article Jean Masamba ma Mpolo introduces into the different parts of the field of indigenous religious traditions in Africa. Here this one article is divided into three parts concerning the issues being addressed. Ma Mpolo's general view is on the relations between indigenous religion in Africa and Christianity. The existence of Islam – though being present in most African societies – as a partner in dialogue was not considered at this time.

6.1.1 Sanctity of life

Jean Masamba ma Mpolo[2]

The first fundamental principle underlying African traditional spirituality and therapeutic practices is the *sanctity of life*. Life comes from God and finds its origin in Him. It must therefore be preserved by all means. Thus, affirmation, preservation and reinforcement of life dominate the theological processes through ways of living in the community and one's capacity to share in the life – to the next generation. If the child is seen by a Rwandese mother as "the field that we share with God", in the Kongo and many other African traditions, the childless woman symbolizes God's continuous creation through meaningful relationships; the childless woman is capable of creating new lives with children of relatives and through her commitment and participation in the welfare of the community. She also becomes mother and true bearer of life and thus shares the sanctity of God's life.

One lives abundant when he/she shares life with others and live in communion with others. *"Bole Bantu, bukaka nsongo"* say the Kongo: "We are people when we live in community; in isolation, we are plague". Among the Kongo, the word *moyo* which can be

---

[1]   In this part of the article: spirituality and counselling for healing and liberation … Masamba ma Mpolo describes special aspects of indigenous religion, in: The Church and Healing. Echoes from Africa, p. 18/19

translated by "soul" or "breath of life", denotes the offspring or descendents. To have *moyo*, therefore, is to be living life in the context of one's community and family. One's life has meaning when it supports and strengthens the collective self. True death in the African context is the exclusion of the individual from the community because of his/her misbehaviours.

This is one of the reasons why many African traditional societies had very elaborated initiation in ceremony. They served as means whereby the adolescents were incorporated into the adult community by going through a symbolic death to childhood, followed by a symbolic birth to adulthood. The death of a disabled-born child was accompanied by a series of rites symbolizing the ritual death of such a child, eliminating the fear of his/her rebirth or reincarnation.

At the end of the rites for initiation ceremonies the young person becomes symbolically a new person. After having learned the ethical demands and the socio-political structure of the community, the young person joins the council of the adults in order to contribute more meaningfully to the well-being of the community. During this period of initiation he/she incorporates into his/her psyche the following basic ontology which undergirds the African social structures, health, political systems and spirituality: "I am, because we are: cognatus, ergo sum."[3]

This is to say that the life of the individual is abundantly lived when it is shared and hidden in the life of his/her community. But this "I am because we are" makes sense when the community can also say: "We are because I am", "We are because he/she is."

6.1.2 Relation between illness, misfortune and sin

Jean Masamba ma Mpolo[4]

This leads me to consider the relationship between illness, misfor-

---

3   John Pobee. African Spirituality ... 1983, 6
4   In this part of the article: spirituality and counselling for healing and liberation ... Masamba ma Mpolo describes special aspects of indigenous religion, in: The Church and Healing. Echoes from Africa, p.19 /20

tune and sin in African traditional spirituality.

At the theoretical and practical levels traditional Africans, in most cases, established a correlation between morality and health, and between sickness and sin.

Illness and misfortune are associated with personal or group transgressions. The illness and death of an older person is accepted as the will of God. The sickness and death of a child, a young person and an active adult, however, considered a disaster and often explained in terms of the result of an offence against the ancestors; violation of social taboos; an attack by deities and evil spirits, or the result of witchcraft.

In African traditional spirituality sin is associated with the breaking of prohibitions agreed on by the community or inherited from the ancestors. The violation of morals leads to a severing of established relationships between God and his creatures, and between the living and the departed ancestors. Certain foods and drinks are prohibited for social and totemic reasons. A good number of taboos involve sexual life. A Kongo widow should not have sexual relations before the ceremonial period of mourning for her deceased husband.

The sense of violation against taboos is very much connected to the feeling of sinning against the Supreme Being. Ancestral spirits, deities, family members and the whole universe are sinned against when taboos are violated. Healing is therefore, seeking liberation from life-negating forces through repentance, confession and reconciliation with all the offended parties.

Traditional healers, family elders and prophets in a number of African Independent Churches organize therapy around the traditional African axiom: illness commonly results from sinful acts. "You have violated a taboo of your clan and this has offended your ancestors. This is why you are sick." Traditional healers and prophets may use divination as one way of ascertaining relationships and broadly naming the shade afflicting the sick person. The identification of the offending agent – even in some broad language – tends to "activate a series of associated ideas producing confession, abreaction, and general catharsis."

6.1.3   Spirits and ancestors in the life of the community

Jean Masamba ma Mpolo[5]

The place occupied by spirits and ancestors in African traditional and many African Independent Church health systems is part of the African spirituality that has to be taken seriously in pastoral care and counselling and other pastoral activities in the Churches in Africa. As indicated earlier, the African cosmology is believed to contain a constellation of powers which constantly interact with human beings and influence, for good or for ill, the course of people's lives.

God, as the creator of life and the power which orders the universe, is best revealed in and through ancestors, lesser deities and spirits. The *Visugu* of Kenya believe that mischievous spirits and divinities may use sorcerers to bring about misfortune, illness and cause death of disobedient family members. Among some African people, when a woman loses several children in succession, it is believed that it is often the same child who returns to punish the mother for some of her misbehaviours or sins committed against a kin member which have not been confessed and atoned for.

These children are believed to belong to a group of evil spirits who spend a short period on earth before returning to their group. These *abiku*, as they are called by the Yoruba, *obanje* by the Igbo, *elima* by the Ngbande or *nsunda* by the Kongo, are given a ritual name as protective measure when they are again born. This prevents from the returning to the other world of the spirits.

Some *Aladura* Churches in Nigeria organize rituals, while some have especial prayers where the protective power of Christ and the Holy Spirit is invoked. Robert Mitchell in his study among the *Aladura* Churches was given another method by an older prophetess. She said that she was able to tie down to earth the *abiku* by

---

[5]   In this part of the article: spirituality and counselling for healing and liberation … Masamba ma Mpolo describes special aspects of indigenous religion, in: The Church and Healing. Echoes from Africa, p. 22

reading Psalms 70 and 91 and praying while burning some candles.

6.1.4   Wholeness in African experience, Christian perspectives

Andrew Olu Igenoza[6]

What is wholeness, especially in African understanding? How are Christians to contend with illness generally, but especially with those illness-types which appear to be mysterious, difficult to diagnose, or stubborn to cure? Why do people in Africa including many who claim to be Christian, feel compelled to go to traditional healers when modern medical facilities are available? What unique contribution can Christians make for the search of wholeness, and what is the ultimate aim in the quest for wholeness?

A consideration of these and allied questions would indicate the importance of the spiritual dimension in the search of wholeness.

This study seeks to emphasize the need to approach the subject of healing among Christians, particularly in Africa, from a holistic perspective with special attention to the spiritual dimension. Inspite of the outstanding achievements of scientific medicine in recent times, most Africans regard it, even at its best, as being non adequate fully for the needs of the situation. This is because of the generally recognizable religious inclination of most Africans, and of their belief in the existence of malevolent spirit-beings and other dangerous, uncanny influences. The validity of African *Weltanschauung* ist left to the individuals to decide after making a critical appraisal of whatever evidence is available. But the prevailing situation still makes it worthwile to consider healing in an African context holistically.

In order to achieve our objective in this paper, we would define wholeness in general terms, and proceed to spotlight what it means in African traditional understanding. A crucial question is whether contemporary Christian experience in any way accords with the

---

[6]   Here are presented parts of the article published in: The Church and Healing. Echoes from Africa, p. 125/6

biblical concept, or whether it has any bearing on the traditional African perception of the matter.

To be whole means to be sound in health, to be complete, un-injured or undamaged. Again it means to be fully restored after an injury, damage or deprivation.

Therefore, wholeness has to do with healing, the total well-being of a person or his or her total restoration in all its dimensions. But it appears that wholeness can mean different things to different people. The definition of health by the World Health Organisation (W.H.O.) is a pointer in this direction. According to this definition, health is "a state of complete physical, mental and social well-being, and not merely the absence of infirmity".

This glaringly overlooks the spiritual dimension to health. But in an African context any definition of health or wholeness must take cognisance of the spiritual. This is because the outlook of the African is fundamentally religious, as has been emphasized by notable scholars. This is a factor which some trained special-ists who administer scientific medical care in Africa often ignore, whereas the traditional medicine-man regards the religious factor as of prime importance. The traditional healer knows that the peo-ple he is dealing with believe in the existence of diverse divini-ties, witches, wizards, the ancestral spirits and other innumerable spirit-beings which are capable of interfering in the affairs of human beings, e.g. by spiritually causing illness. The traditional medicine man who may also be a diviner equally knows that his client be-lieves in the efficacy of divination, magic, sacrifice, incantation, in-vocation, encantment and the herbal preparations with which he seeks to help them. He believes that these spiritual realities have vi-tal roles to play in matters of sickness and restoration of health. In the context of the traditional African, sickness is not only a physical disharmony but also it "has spiritual, religious, medical and socio-ethical dimensions."

Thus, if a sick person came to the traditional diviner-healer with a complaint, the latter would first of all find out through dialogue and divination, the possible "causes" of the trouble; he would ad-vise, prescibe sacrifices and rituals to be performed in seeking a remedy. In the context of blood sacrifice and meal offerings before a shrine, the sick person with his community would pray, confess guilt and effect reconciliation both with the living and the departed. There could also be rituals of exorcism to drive away, or bring under control, the spirits that may be afflicting the patient or community. In addition to all these, there would be actual herbal medication.

This traditional approach, no doubt, is holistic and goes a long way in giving psychological and spiritual relief to those who believe and participate in it. It is this holistic approach in traditional healing practice with its emphasis on the spiritual, the ethical and the social which makes it highly commendable.

6.2 Approaches

Ulrike Elsdörfer

In order to get a first glimpse on the indigenous world-view in Africa, one has to reflect upon four very important issues of African philosophy and religion. Its anthropology aims at four qualities:

Wholeness

"To be whole means to be sound in health, to be complete, uninjured or undamaged. Again it means to be fully restored after an injury, damage or deprivation.

Therefore, wholeness has to do with healing, the total well-being of a person or his or her total restoration in all its dimensions. But it appears that wholeness can mean different things to different people."[7]

Healing

"This glaringly overlooks the spiritual dimension to health. But in an African context any definition of health or wholeness must take cogni-

---

[7] s. Igenoza

sance of the spiritual. This is because the outlook of the African is fundamentally religious, as has been emphasized by notable scholars. This is a factor which some trained specialists who administer scientific medical care in Africa often ignore, whereas the traditional medicine-man regards the religious factor as of prime importance. The traditional healer knows that the people he is dealing with believe in the existence of diverse divinities, witches, wizards, the ancestral spirits and other innumerable spirit-beings which are capable of interfering in the affairs of human beings, e.g. by spiritually causing illness. The traditional medicine man who may also be a diviner equally knows that his client believes in the efficacy of divination, magic, sacrifice, incantation, invocation, encantment and the herbal preparations with which he seeks to help them."[8]

Community

"One lives abundant when he/she shares life with others and live in communion with others. *"Bole Bantu, bukaka nsongo"* say the Kongo: "We are people when we live in community; in isolation, we are plague". Among the Kongo, the word *moyo* which can be translated by "soul" or "breath of life", denotes the offspring or descendents. To have *moyo*, therefore, is to be living life in the context of one's community and family. One's life has meaning when it supports and strengthens the collective self. True death in the African context is the exclusion of the individual from the community because of his/her misbehaviours."[9]

Spirituality

"Africa has always been a spiritual terrain. The wind is blowing"[10] – these are the concluding words of a lecture Wilhelmina Kalu, an African pastoral psychologist and theologian from Nigeria, gave in Nordwijkerhout 1991. In trying to understand African people and even to implement western ideas of psychology on them one has to consider the close connections of man and the spirit world as well

---

[8] s. Igenoza
[9] s. Mpolo
[10] Wilhelmina Kalu: Gospel and pastoral counselling in Africa, in: Pastoral Care and Context, p. 114

as the dense relations of man and nature. "The missionaries feared the problem of control in the move of the Holy Spirit and the spiritist character of the existing African religiosity".[11] Shorter, a Catholic theologian in Africa, tried to seek for a path of dialogue between Christian and African spiritualities and by that for a liturgical renewal of the Catholic church in Africa. But traditional churches are not as successsful in these efforts.

White churches deriving from missionaries' activities suffer from low growth rate, while a "creative spirituality" attracts African people. Theology, if it wants to be accepted and successful in Africa, has to consider all those texts of the New Testament, which address pneumatical issues and which normally are neglected in many other parts of the world.

By this, Kalu states, "it must be quickly added that the Gospel is not Christianity. The Gospel is like the inside nut of the coconut."[12] But as in the early times of the biblical texts, surroundings have to be considered and well-understood, in order to place the contents of the Gospel in a reasonable way.

And for the African spirituality water, earth, and even space is filled with spirits, deriving from the human world, but existing in their own right. These spirits have to be considered in every moment, and an interpretation of religion has to implement them on a prominent place. The forementioned evil spirits coming back only for a short time – to be reborn in an ill child, for instance – result from the former lives of unlucky persons who have died a "bad death". This means: death by suicide, death in early age, death by accident or lightning; having "a good death" means to die in old age and not to return to life in order to not to disturb the life of the descendants. Good ancestors only come back in order to give advice or blessings or to be mediators in conflicts.

Different natural spheres as water or the realm beneath the earth are part of the entire surroundings of African people. Spirits inhabit these regions, having their special fights according to their individ-

---

[11] s. a., p. 100
[12] s. a., p. 101

ual characters. "But this world-view is a precarious vision of human existence as it perceives a world under siege by evil spirits. Human beings oblate, propitiate and seek the powers of the beneficiant gods to ward off the attacks of the evil powers, to enhance the battle of existence and to control space-time events. It is an alive universe. It recognizes the hidden warfare underneath the material, existential life."[13]

There is no dichotomy between the sacred and profane. Spirituality is an all-embracing concept, it represents an alternative to western medicine, as Hollenweger[14] says, it gives explorations on the "dark side of the soul"[15].

So for a psychological trained counsellor it is difficult to seize the moment when the interwoven net gives some space and a chance for a change. Counsellors using western pychological methods always have to take into consideration the spiritual implications of unknown traditions (as witchcraft and knowledge deriving from the use of herbal medicine), and the coexistence of both world-views has to be considered.

Altogether, this is what Kalu states concerning her experience and the situation in Africa in the 1990s. "It is important to note that the fast growth rate in Church membership in Africa ensures that all the models co-exist and there are many more in development. The pastoral counsellor is careful no to disappoint in the spiritual search of the individual. Those who are dissatisfied move to the spiritist churches and to traditional healers to participate in a host of sacrificial rituals and 'special' prayers."[16]

---

[13] s. a., p. 103
[14] In: Wilhelmina Kalu, p. 107
[15] s. a.
[16] Kalu, p. 113

7 The global ICPCC movement: Documents

7.1 The Risks of Freedom: The 1st International Congress on Pastoral Care and Counselling, 8th – 15th August 1979, Edinburgh/Scotland

The Church of Scotland

General Assembly

July 28, 1979

It is exceedingly interesting and important news for all of us in Scotland that the first World Congress on Pastoral Care and Counselling is to be held in Edinburgh in August of this year.

My mind goes back to the great ecumenical gatherings held in Edinburgh in 1910 and 1937. In both of these meetings Scottish churchmen played a prominent part, and both had a large influence on our people. No doubt the same will be true this year. But more important than that is the emerge of a world movement which will enable us all to understand and serve one another better in a time of constant and perplexing change. Many people in Scotland will be wishing you well and praying for the success of your gathering. It gives me the greatest pleasure to send to the Congress the greetings of the General Assembly of the Church of Scotland, and to assure you of our continued interest and concern.

Robin Barbour

Moderator

At this congress "THE NEWSLETTER of the International Committee for Pastoral Care and Counselling" was established
Editors: Heije Faber – Maarn, Holland
Denis Duncan – London, Britain
Elizabeth Kilbourn – Toronto, Canada
Teunis Kruijne – Groningen, Holland
President of ICPCC was: Werner Becher, Frankfurt/Germany 1979-1983
Vice-President: John H. Patton, Atlanta, Georgia, USA 1979-1983
Chair of the First International Congress on Pastoral Care and Counselling in Edinburgh 1979 was Reverend Denis Duncan.

7.2   Symbol and Story in Pastoral Care and Counselling: The 2nd International Congress of ICPCC in San Francisco 1983: A letter from the President Werner Becher[1]

Dear friends in many countries of the world,

We are on route to our Second International Congress on Pastoral Care and Counselling. In 1983 we shall meet in San Francisco. Our theme "Symbol and Story in Pastoral Care and Counselling" will challenge us to share our different experiences and understandings of our work as rabbis, priests, ministers and pastors, as counsellors and therapists. We shall also discover how many treasures of our Jewish and Christian traditions and our contemporary life we have in common despite our theological, cultural, social and political differences.

I look forward with great expectations to our encounter with new and our reunion with old friends.

My expectations for our congress in the United States are greater than for any of our previous international conferences. I have learned much from our American colleagues since my Clinical Pastoral Education in Topeka 1970/71, and I know that many of you like me have enriched our pastoral

---

[1]   First published in: THE NEWSLETTER No. 2 – Fall 1982

care and teaching with the help of our American friends. The "living human documents" in many countries of the world have gained from the American approach to pastoral care and counselling.

I also should like our friends in the United States and in Canada to know how much we appreciate all their preparations for our congress in San Francisco. Since the decision of our International Committee in 1979 in Edinburgh to hold our next congress in North America I have observed not only the well known American efficiency but also the love and hope of our North American friends are investing to host us in their country.

Many of you in other countries are involved in preparing our meeting in San Franzisco, too. Our membership associations in the United Kingdom and in West Germany hold national conferences on the theme "Symbol and Story in Pastoral Care and Counselling".

The Second European Conference in September 1981 at the Catholic University of Lublin in Poland on "Religious Values and Experiences in Pastoral Care and Counselling" was an important step on our way to San Francisco. I shall never forget the enormous concern of our Polish friends for the spiritual wellbeing of their people. In this Newletter a participant from East Germany where the first European Conference took place in 1977 and a colleague from Finland where the Third European Conference will be convened in 1985 are reporting and reflecting on their experiences in Lublin.

The first Asian Conference in June 1982 in Manila discussed the needs and concerns of pastoral care and counselling in the churches of Asia. Two of our colleagues in Asia share with you some of their experiences and insights. I was particularly impressed by the large number of women representing Roman Catholic religious orders at this conference in the Philippines. It was important for me to experience belonging to a minority, as our friends coming from countries in the Third World world usually do at our conferences. I am afraid, it will not be different in San Franzisco.

Of course, our way from Edinburgh to San Francisco has not been free from difficulties. At the first meeting of our International Committee we could not overlook the fact that the national organisations had only delegated Protestant, white, male representatives. The cooption of a rabbi from North America, two friends from Africa and two women from Canada and the United States was certainly only a first attempt to improve this

171

situation. At the second meeting of our committee in Lublin our Roman Catholic friend from Poland and our two friends from the Philippines, Japan and Australia joined our committee. I hope that the International Council on Pastoral Care and Counselling which is to be convened in San Francisco will be more representative in terms of cultural backgrounds, religious affiliation and sex, and I request the national organisations to consider this point when appointing their new representatives.

Since my appointment as president of our International Committee my family has been willing to arrange our holidays according to my wishes, and my church has given me the time and money to visit many of you in North and Latin America, Africa, Asia and Europe. I have been able to travel to the United States and Cuba, to Jamaica, to England and Scotland, to the German Democratic Republic, Greece, Holland, Norway, Poland and Switzerland, to Japan, Taiwan and the Philippines. I write this letter in South Africa, before I continue my journey to Zimbabwe and Tanzania. Wherever I visited I was impressed by the similarities of human suffering and growth. Of course, the attempts to help through pastoral care and counselling vary from country to country, from community to community, from church to church. I was particularly moved by the pastoral care through words and deeds, through listening to each other and to the word of God, through communal prayers and intercessions in areas of extreme poverty and of political tensions. The holistic approach in pastoral care is obviously requiring more than only the care for individual needs in mind, body and spirit. We have to discover how we can help and learn to help in the context of our world.

May God help us with that task when we meet in 1983 in San Francisco!

SHALOM   Werner Becher

7.3   A brief history of the Asian Conference on Pastoral Care and Counseling

Narciso C. Dumalagan

The Clinical Pastoral Education program was first inaugurated in the Philippines on June 7th, 1965[2]. The founder of this program was J. Albert Dalton, an American Episcopal Missionary to the Philippines. Through his determined zeal to see if CPE training would be useful in Asia, particularly the Philippines, he began to organize the Philippine Association for Clinical Pastoral Care (PACPC). This organzation was established with the cooperation of various agencies. There were the hospital administrator, the medical director, the nursing service director, all of St. Luke's Medical Center; there were the deans of St. Andrews Theological Seminary, Union Theological Seminary, Divinity School of Silliman University, College of Theology of the Philippine Central University, and the Lutheran Seminary of the Philippines.[3]

Among with this key agencies were the executive secretary of the United Church of Christ in the Philippines (UCCP), the Bishop of the Philippine Epsicopal Church, and the executive director of the Inter-Church Commission on Medical Care with its head office at the National Council of Churches in the Philippines (NCCP). They were the agencies actively involved and which participated in the establishment of the Clinical Pastoral Education in the country.

Since June 7th, 1965 the CPE Program up to the present offers not only clinical pastoral education training for religious, clergies, seminarians, and lay people but also pastoral care and counselling services. The CPE is open not only to Filipinos and other Asian students but also to applicants from other non – Asian countries.

---

[2]   Dumalagan, N.C., Becher, W. and Taniguchi, T.(Eds), Pastoral Care and Counseling in Asia: Its Needs and Concerns, Manila: CPCAP publication (1983), p. 45

[3]   Ibid.

It was from this pastoral organization background that this writer from the Philippines was invited to attend the 1ˢᵗ International Congress on Pastoral Care and Counselling (ICPCC) held in Edinburgh, Scotland in 1979.[4] Two years later a European continental conference on Pastoral Care and Counselling was held in Lublin, Poland in 1981. Two Asian representatives were invited to attend both the European Conference and the ICPCC officers' meeting. These Asians were Taizo Taniguchi of Japan and Narciso C. Dumalagan of the Philippines. They served as observers from Asia as the ICPCC Council discussed global expansion of pastoral care and counselling with the hope that eventually each country will be represented in the Council. They also planned the details of the second International Congress on Pastoral Care and Counselling to be held in San Francisco, California, on the theme "Telling Your Stories."

One of the major concerns of the ICPCC was to identify countries that already have a national organization and invited a representative from that country to attend the ICPCC assembly with the possibility that they will also organize a Pastoral Care and Counselling movement in their respective continents. Identified persons in countries that have no national organizations on pastoral care and counselling are also invited so that they can organize a national association on pastoral care and continue to participate and contribute its pastoral resources in the International Congress.

The Asian representatives to the ICPCC Planning Committee in Poland were asked if they would be willing to organize a conference on pastoral care and counselling in Asia. The Asians felt positive with the suggestions. The Council then, and this was accepted by the Asian delegates, designated Dumalagan as the convenor of the first Asian conference on Pastoral Care and Counselling and Taniguchi as the Secretary. The Council offered a token amount of funds to help start the birthing of the first Asian Conference on Pastoral Care and Counselling (ACPCC).

On June 11ᵗʰ-14ᵗʰ, 1982, the First Asian Conference was convened. It was held in Metro Manila, Philippines. This was hosted

---

[4] Ibid., p. 151

by the Clinical Pastoral Care Association of the Philippines (CP-CAP), formerly Philippine Association for Clinical Pastoral Care (PACPC). This was jointly sponsored by the CPCAP and the ICPCC. This was attended by 86 participants from 12 Asian Countries and a few non – Asian representatives from North America and Europe. The proceedings of this conference were published by the CPCAP in 1983 edited by Dumalagan, Becher and Taniguchi. The theme of the conference was "Pastoral Care and Counselling in Asia: Its Needs and Concerns". It attempted to survey existing pastoral care and counselling activities in various Asian countries. It also tried to search expressions of concern and interest in the area of pastoral care and counselling in respective nations.[5]

The second Asian Conference was held in Tokyo, Japan, on July 3rd- 6th, 1984. It was decided in the first Asian conference to hold the Asian conference every two years. The Tokyo conference was sponsored by an Ecumenical Planning Committee of 15 members chaired by Philip Ohara. But the initial backing and administrative promotion were provided by the Personal Growth and Counselling Center of the Japan Lutheran Theological College. The theme was "Current Challenges on Pastoral Care and Counselling in Asia". Both Roman Catholics and Protestants were represented among the conference participants.[6] The proceedings of the conference were published by the Second Asian Conference on Pastoral Care and Counselling and the Personal Growth and Counselling Center in Tokyo, Japan.

In the spirit of uninterrupted continuity, the Third Asian Conference was held in New Delhi, India, on January 23rd–26th, 1986. This was convened by Salim Sharif of Sandarshan Institute for Counselling Personal Growth. The theme was "The Family".[7] The Sandarshan Institute Team and the India Association of Pastoral Care and Counselling hosted the conference. Representatives from seven Asian countries actively participated along with a large number

---

[5]   Ibid, p. VIII

[6]   Dale, Kenneth,ed., The 2nd Asian Conference on Pastoral Care and Counseling, Tokyo: ACPCC pub., (1994), p. 3

[7]   Sharif, Salim: Third Asian Conference on Pastoral Care and Counseling program, New Delhi: (1986) p. 4

from the national field. Its obejctives were to provide an opportunity for professionals of different countries in Asia to interact, educate, sensitize, enlighten and increase understanding of the family in this changing society.[8]

The 4th Asian conference proposed to take place in South Korea in 1988. This was planned after the 3rd conference in India. This plan did not push through due to prevailing activities taking place in Korea in that year. Through Kenneth Dale's consultation with Narciso Dumalagan, other countries, including Japan, were asked if they would like to host the 4th Asian conference. There being no other country willing to host and finding Japan to be a very expensive country to have a conference, the Philippines accepted a second round of hosting the 4th Asian Conference on July 24th–28th, 1989. This was sponsored by the Pastoral Care Foundation of the Philippines (PCFP), formerly CPCAP. The theme was "Ministry to the Aging in Changing Asian Family Values". The objectives of this conference were to heighten awareness of Asian resources in ministering to the elderly in Asian society; to deepen understanding and appreciation of the uniqueness of caring for the elderly in Asia; and to recognize existing problems faced by the elderly in Asia continent.

This was attended by 142 participants representing 13 countries including a representative from the United States. The countries were: Australia, Hong Kong, Indonesia, India, Korea, Malaysia, Pakistan, Papua New Guinea, Singapore, Vietnam and the Philippines.[9]

During the 4th Asian conference, Singapore was asked if they would be interested to host the 5th Asian conference. The representatives of Singapore considered the offer positively but subject for approval of Singapore by the body of pastoral care people in Singapore. Salim Sharif strongly suggested to write and ask Mesach Krisetya of Indonesia if they would like to host the 5th Asian Conference. After a few month Mesach Krisetya of Indonesia wrote and

---

[8]   Third ACPCC Report, New Delhi: (1986), p. 1
[9]   Espino, Jose Ms., Ministry to the Aging in Changing Asian Familiy Values, Manila: (1989), p. 108

informed that they accepted to host the 5th Asian Conference. But with Indonesia having accepted first, Singapore gave in and looked forward to the 6th Asian Conference in Singapore.

Shortly after the ICPCC Congress in Amsterdam, Ronald Cross of Australia wrote to inform Dumalagan that Australia would like to host the 6th or 7th Asian Conference. This was another inspiring offer from a country whose representation in all Asian conferences had always been responsive.

The history of the Asian Conference on Pastoral Care and Counselling achieved a firmer and clearer vision when all the Asian representatives attending the ICPCC in the Netherlands in 1991, met and elected the Asian Council and Office Bearers. Elected were: Mesach Krisetya (Indonesia) – President, Narciso C. Dumalagan (Philippines – Vice President, and J. A. Trisna (Indonesia) – Secretary/Treasurer. The Council members were: Ronald Cross (Australia), James Tan (Singapore), Liam MC. Cannon (Korea), Tsugikazu Nishigaki (Japan), and David Shakuntala (India). Salim Sharif took the responsibility of getting the Newsletter formulated for the Asian Network.

The Indian delegation felt the possibility of hosting the 6th ICPCC in Asia in 1999 and thought that India would be a good place. Sharif offered to work on this. Proposal and report on this plan will be taken up at the next Asian conference in Indonesia[10] on August 1993. The venue of this assembly is Bali.

7.4 History and Context of the ICPCC

James Farris[11]

This chapter will focus on the history of the ICPCC (International Council on Pastoral Care and Counseling – www.icpcc.net/), and

---

[10] Minutes of The Asian Group Meeting, Prepared by David Shakuntala, Nordwijkerhout: (August 4, 1991) p. 1

[10] Dr. James Farris is professor at the Methodist University in Sao Paolo/Brazil

will discuss the themes of Communion, Pastoral Care and Counseling, Mutual Respect, and Spiritual Care. I will speak in the first person, because these are my personal memories and impressions during 15 years of participation in the International Council. The first thing that I want to present is a short summary of the history of pastoral care and counseling, and the integration of the vision and history of the ICPCC. All of these contents can be found on the Internet Site of the ICPCC, but what is important is to examine the integrity between the vision or mission statement of the ICPCC, and how it has respected these values.

Let me begin by reflecting on the complexity of this mission, or vision. The ICPCC is different from many other groups that discuss the identity of Pastoral Care and Counseling, or Spiritual Care. This difference is the importance of respecting and integrating a variety of cultural and individual perspectives. This has not always been easy. What is justice? What is Care? What is Pastoral Care and Counseling? What is Mutual Respect? These are not easy questions, but this is the genius of the ICPCC. Thought its history, it has sought to discuss these themes in open and honest ways.

At this point it is important to remember the recent history of Pastoral Care and Counseling. During the 1950's, 60's and the beginning of the 1970's Pastoral Care and Counseling was dominated by the influence of Psychology. I will not discuss the influences of Sigmund Freud and Carl Jung. They are profound, and beyond the scope of this discussion. Leaving Freud and Jung aside, in the United States, the influence was largely via the Humanistic Psychology of Carl Rodgers (Rodgers, 1967) and Abraham Maslow (Maslow, 1959). As well as the eclectic perspective of Rollo May (May, 1972) Pastoral Care and Counseling was also influence by various Neo-Freudians, including Viktor Frankl (Frankl,) Erich Fromm (Fromm, 1951) and Donald Winnicott (Winnicott, 1974) There are, of course, many other influences. These are only a few of the possible examples and influences.

In England this was not radically different, but the influence was more via psychoanalysis. One text that portrays the evolution of Pastoral Care and Counseling in England is the book *The Tree of*

Healing (Hurding, 1985). I am not familiar with the evolution of Pastoral Care and Counseling in Europe, but one of the best texts written by a German author, that was teaching in the South of Brasil at the time is *Teologia Prática: No Contexto da América Latina*, Christoph Schneider-Harppecht (Schneider-Harppecht, 1998) regarding the History of Practical Theology, which leads to the conclusion that Pastoral Care and Counseling in Brasil was highly influenced by North American and European traditions.

Still, the classic texts that outlines the development of Pastoral Care and Counseling, and Pastoral Theology are *A History of the Cure of Souls* (McNeill, 1951), *The Ministry in Historical Perspective* (Niebuhr and Williams, 1956) and *Pastoral Care in Historical Perspective* (Clebsch and Jaekle, 1975).

This does not mean that there have not been conflicts between cultures and individual personalities. There have been many conflicts, and will continue to be. However, this only adds to the richness of the dialogues that the ICPCC offers between all of the complex elements involved.

On a separate, but related, note, there has been a certain historical interface, and at times conflict, between the ICPCC and the SIPCC (Society for Intercultural Pastoral Care and Counseling). This is a very complex subject, but has to do with the origins of the two institutions in Germany, and that in many moments the two groups shared the same members and leadership. Both have been led by individuals and groups with very strong beliefs and personalities, and the interchange of leadership and shared goals has, at times, led to conflicts and misunderstandings. Nonetheless, the two groups maintain their individual identities, missions, and practical objectives.

This is not the space to discuss the similarities and differences between the two groups. However, it is enough to say that while both share similar objectives; they are like two drops of water in an immense ocean. There is more than enough space for both.

What follows is a copy of the content of the site of the ICPCC regarding the objectives and history of Congresses. What is interesting at this point is to recognize the congruence of the objectives and the themes of the Congresses. While the Objectives are rather broad, they always return to the themes of Pastoral Care and Counseling, Inclusion, Education, Justice, and Responsibility. While it is obvious that these are very complex theme, within and between cultures this is one of the fundamental marks of the ICPCC; to deal with the complexities and, at times, differences between various theories and practices of Pastoral Care and Counseling.

Objectives

ICPCC represents a truly international, ecumenical and proactive movement of women and men desiring to respond to current needs and situations faced by real life people in the world through the skills and mediations of pastoral care and counselling.

The Council serves as a 'web-like' network of people to
- help promote the reflective practice of Pastoral Care and Counselling throughout the world
- inform, educate and inspire practitioners of Pastoral Care and Counselling in every place
- enable practitioners to be in touch with each other and to learn from good practice wherever it occurs
- to oversee the running of "International Congresses" every four years.

The International Council came into existence in 1979 at the first International Congress of reflective practitioners of Pastoral Care and Counselling held in Edinburgh, Scotland.

There had been gatherings from as early as 1972 of various European and American practitioners but Edinburgh 1979, where over four hundred people from all the continents gathered, was a watershed for Pastoral Care and Counseling akin to the ecumenical mission and church meetings of 1910 and 1937.

Historically and actually, the concepts of Pastoral Care and Counseling, or Spiritual Care, raise various complex and challenging questions. For example: What is the fundamental identity of Pastoral Care and Counseling? What is "Spiritual Care"? How do cultural contexts affect these two complex concepts? There are, obviously, no simple answers to these complex questions, but these are the questions that the ICPCC deals with.

ICPCC represents a truly international, ecumenical and proactive movement of women and men desiring to respond to current needs and situations faced by real life people in the world through the skills and mediations of pastoral care and counselling.

The Council serves as a 'web-like' network of people to help promote the reflective practice of Pastoral Care and Counselling throughout the world

1. inform, educate and inspire practitioners of Pastoral Care and Counselling in every place
2. enable practitioners to be in touch with each other and to learn from good practice wherever it occurs.

The concept Inter-Faith can be easily confused with Inter-Religious dialogue, which generally deals with questions of how to communicate between different religious traditions. Inter-Religious dialogue deals with how to approach practical, ethical and theological experiences between, for example, Christianity and Buddhism. Inter-Faith is a broader term. Assuming that faith involves the construction of universes of meaning, it includes both Inter-Religious and Inter-Denominational communication, or dialogue. Inter-Faith includes how to share experiences between both different Religious and Denominational traditions. This is important because it points to the central place of dialogue between Religions and Denominations within Religious Traditions.

A previous version of this part of the discussion was published in: Daniel S. Schipaini e Leah Dawn Buchert (eds). *Interfaith Spritual Care: Understandings and Practices*. Kirthner, Ontário, Canada, Pandora Press, 2009. This introduction is original, but is based on the original text.

Spirituality is another complex concept. However, in order to avoid the seemingly infinite discussions regarding what is Spirituality, I will use a fairly simple, and classic, understanding of the term. Spirituality is the creation and fostering of Communion between persons, groups, creation, and God. What this means and how to do it is incredibly complex, and varies widely between Religions and Denominations. However, the essence, or ground, of Spirituality seems to always return to one central question: "How do we create, foster, and live in Communion-Community with ourselves, our neighbor, our world, and our God?"

The idea of Communion may be the key to this discussion. Communion is an ideal, much like the Kingdom of God. Communion suggests basic, even if very general, shared values, beliefs, understandings of who we are as human beings, what we believe to be true, and our images of God. However, such an ideal is often far from what we experience in day-to-day life. Human values, beliefs, understandings of who we are, what is true, and our images of God are incredibly diverse. This diversity often creates conflicts and can shatter Communion. When Communion is fragmented by the diversity of experiences and beliefs, Inter-Faith Spiritual Care is very difficult.

The word "Communion" suggests "Community". To live in Community means living with, and hopefully respecting the beliefs of the "Other". Community generally refers to the kind and quality of relationships that we offer to each another, or, in other words, how we can best live together. It assumes that what we have, what we can offer, and who we are can be, at least to some degree, held in common. This does not mean that we live in an ideal world where everything is held in common. Community means that we recognize that we are not islands unto ourselves.

The opposite of community is immunity. To be immune means that we are protected from the dangerous "Other", or from that which could threaten to infect us. Who we are and what is ours, is ours, and we do not need to share. Or, at best, we can share with those that serve our needs. Immunity implies a certain kind of community, but one which is finally self-serving. As long as the "Other" serves our needs, there is no threat. They can be part of our circle of relationships. However, when they disagree with us, or pose some sort of threat, they can be quickly dismissed, or defined as the enemy. The highest values in immunity are safety and security.

When Communion-Community directs our lives and faith, Inter-Faith Spiritual Care can be a living reality because it invites living together, sharing, and, at least, minimal mutual respect. To care for the "Other" is not a threat. It becomes a part of who we are, and how we live together.

When immunity guides our lives, it is much more difficult to live together, share, and respect one another. The "Other" can become a source of infection, or a threat. One of the fundamental questions for Inter-Faith Spiritual Care may be exactly at this point. When and where do we feel at peace with caring for the "Other", who may have values, beliefs, and faith that are very different from ours? Who is the "Other"? How secure are we in our own beliefs? What are the limits of our understanding of "Communion" and "Community"?

The word "God" immediately raises problems, because Spirituality, in its broadest sense, does not necessarily include Western concepts of "God", and religious traditions often understand "God", or Imago Dei, in ways that are quite different. However, since Inter-Faith is a broad and inclusive concept, it is well worth considering that, in the words of Paul Tillich, the concept of "God" reveals and expresses our "ultimate concern".[12] God does not necessarily reflect the beliefs of any one Religious Tradition, but is that which organizes, orients and expresses our deepest beliefs and values. "God" is the "ground of our being", and orients our life, and the meaning of Communion and Community. This is one of the foundations of the ICPCC.

This is very similar to the idea of Rudolf Otto that "God" reflects a universal human experience that is A Priori.[13] It is a part of our consciousness. The possibility of experiencing the "Mysterium Tremendum et Fascinans", The Mystery, The Power and The Attraction of the Infinite, is built into our existence. How we experience and express this deep reality varies enormously, but it is there. It is always a presence and potential. Inter-Faith Spiritual Care respects this presence and potential in all of its complexity and variety.

Once again we return to the question of Communion, Commu-

---

[12] Paul Tillich. *Dynamics of Faith*. New York, Harper Torchbooks, 1953.
[13] Rudolf Otto: The idea of the holy

nity and Identity. How my community understands God, or the Infinite, and how another community understands God, or the Infinite, are often very different. What are the limits of our tolerance for differences of belief, liturgy, and action? How do we deal with these differences? What does "Communion" mean? What does "Community" mean? How can we offer Spiritual Care to those who believe in ways that we do not understand, and can even frighten us?

Finally, Care is how our community seeks to create, foster and live in Communion and Community, in practical terms. Or, in other words, how is it that we seek to live in such ways that are faithful to our beliefs about the nature, presence, and will of God, and at the same time live with those that believe in ways that may be very different? Within various Monotheistic traditions, Care is intimately related to the Care of Souls. Traditionally, it includes healing, sustaining, guiding, reconciling, and educating. It is an expression of deep mutual correction, encouragement, and solidarity which embraces the totality of life. In this case, the term "Care of Souls" refers to the totality and integrity of human beings in light of the nature of the Divine. Who is included and who is excluded in the "Care of Souls", Communion, and Community is a key question in Inter-Faith Spiritual Care.

Finally, the ideal of Inter-Faith Spiritual Care seeks to create and foster Communion and Community between persons of diverse religious traditions and denominations. Since the beginning of the ICPCC, this has been a fundamental question. It is how we express the Love of God, the Ground of our Being, both within our Communities of Faith, and beyond them. If there is one question that dominates Inter-Faith Spiritual Care it is: "How do we build bridges, and at the same time maintain and respect our own identity and community of faith?" There are, of course, no simple answers.

Brazilian Contexts

In order to understand Inter-Faith Spiritual Care, or Pastoral Care and Counseling, in Brazil, it is important to have some notion of Brazilian Culture. To begin with, that there is no one "Brazilian Perspective" or "Culture". Brazil is physically the size of the United States, and is composed of a seemingly infinite variety of cultures. Historically, the south of Brazil was influenced by German and Italian immigrations. The north of Brazil maintains African influences. The Amazon continues to reflect strong indigenous influences. The central regions of Brazil are a mixture of a wide variety of cultural influences that include European, South American and Portuguese traditions. The major urban centers are a seemingly infinite mixture of cultures and traditions, currently highly influenced by North American and European values. It is impossible to understand Brazilian cultures without taking into account the political, economic and religious influence of Portugal, Europe, and the United States in the last 500 years. Specifically, the religious "map" of Brazil has been, and continues to be, profoundly influenced by each of these.

This is the link to the current religious context of Brazil. Beginning in the 1500's, Brazil was almost exclusively Roman Catholic. Indigenous religious expressions were repressed, and almost systematically eradicated. This situation did not change significantly until the mid 1800's, with the arrival of various Protestant missionaries, generally from the United States and Europe. These new "religious expressions" were generally tolerated by the Roman Catholic Church. This was due, in great degree, to the perception that these "religious groups", or "sects", generally concentrated their attention and ministry on members of their own group. For example, Methodist, Baptist, Lutheran, Presbyterian, Adventist, and Mennonite missionaries and pastors typically ministered to members of their own communities. The tendency was to Care for one's own group.

However, as these "religious groups" began to grow and expand, this attitude changed. Beginning in the 1930's and 1940's Protestant traditions began to have an increasingly important presence in Brazilian culture. This presence was religious, economic, social, and educational. This represented a shift in power, or social presence. While the Roman Catholic Church was still the dominant religious presence in Brazil, it was no longer the only Church in Brazil. This shift in religious power, presence and expression was further complicated by the resurgence, in roughly the same period, of Indigenous and African religious traditions that had been effectively underground, but still very powerful, for centuries. By the 1960's, the religious map of Brazil had changed radically.

To further complicate the situation, the relatively small groups of Pentecostals, which had been present in Brazil since the 1920's, began to grow rapidly in the 1950's and 1960's. In the 1970's and 1980's a new expression of Pentecostalism, Neo-Pentecostalism, also began to grow rapidly. It is difficult to describe Neo-Pentecostalism. As a movement, it is neither Pentecostal nor Protestant. It is influenced by the Theology of Prosperity, marketing theory, and a mixture of Roman Catholic, Pentecostal, Protestant, and Afro-Brazilian theologies. Its growth, over the past twenty years, has been phenomenal.

In summary, in terms of formal church membership, according to the 1960, 1971, 1980, 1991 and 2000 Brazilian census[14]:

This "informal" map is made even more complex by the reality that many "church members" also frequent other religious worship services. Once again, this refelects the complexity of the task of the ICPPC, and the challenges of its mission statement. The result is that there is tremendous competition between religious traditions for membership, or, more specifically, for financial support. What was, more or less fifty years ago, a Roman Catholic country has become an incredibly diverse and competitive religious universe.

To give some life to these numbers and this history, I would like to give an informal example of the religious diversity in Brazil. I live in a middle class neighborhood in São Bernardo do Campo, one of the many cities that surround São Paulo, which is the second or third largest city in the world, with a population of approximately 12 million.

In front of my home there is an Umbanda House Church (an Afro-Brazilian religion). Up the street is an independent Pentecostal

---

[14] A.F. Pierucci. Bye bye Brasil: O Declínio das Religiões Tradicionais no Censo de 2000. *Estudos Avançados*, v. 18, n. 52, pp. 1-12, 2005.

(Total membership exceeds 100% because of multiple – church membership, which is not uncommon in Brazil.)

	1960	1971	1980	1991	2000
Roman Catholic	93.1%	91.8%	89%	83.3%	73.9%
Historical Protestant*	4%	5.2%	10%	11%	20.6%
Pentecostal	?	?	3.2%	6%	10.6%
Neo-Pentecostal**	?	?	?	?	?
Afro-Brazilian / Other Religions***	?	4.5%	4.4%	7.8%	6.6%

* Baptist, Adventist, Lutheran, Presbyterian, Methodist, Congregational and Mennonites.
** Statistics regarding membership in Neo-Pentecostal Churches is very difficult to determine due to the lack of formal membership records.
*** Kardecista, Umbanda, Candomblé, Neo-Christian Religions such as Jehovah's Witness, Mormons and Good Will League, and all other recognized religious groups.

Store – Front Church. Within a one mile radius of my home are: a Roman Catholic Church – which occupies a central place in the neighborhood square; one Candomblé center (an Afro-Brazilian religion); two Neo-Pentecostal Churches; six independent Pentecostal Churches; two Japanese religious centers; one Mormon Temple; one Methodist Church; one House Church which I cannot identify, and; the Methodist School of Theology in Brazil. I have cable television, which is still a rarity in Brazil, but an influence that is both powerful and growing. Amidst the 34 channels that I receive, one is owned by the Roman Catholic Church, one by the Universal Church of the Kingdom of God (a Neo- Pentecostal Church), and one by the Rebirth in Christ Church (a Neo- Pentecostal Church). I do not have statistics regarding the number of independent religious programs broadcast on various channels, but it is an impressive presence. The number of formal and independent – illegal religious radio stations is very difficult to calculate, but probably numbers in the hundreds.

In summary, religion in Brazil is very present, incredibly diverse, and highly competitive. This is not to say that religious diversity is something new, or exclusive to Brazil. Religious diversity and competition is a widespread phenomenon in the modern world. What marks the situation in Brazil are the complex interactions between social – economic context, the historical concentration of power in one religious tradition, and the current growth of some traditions in the midst of the near stagnation of others. These realities profoundly influence relations between Religious Traditions and Denominations. These are at least some of the religious – social contexts that influence the question of Inter-Faith Spiritual Care.

The ICPCC is alive and well amidst the very complicated religious life and beliefs of various cultures. This is not to say that the ICPCC will resolve all of these complexities. That is not the goal of the ICPCC. We are seeking to establish a dialogue between different cultures and contexts. That is the contribution of the ICPCC.

7.5   Personal Growth and Counseling Center of the Lutheran Theological College and Seminary

3-10-20, Osawa, Mitaka, Tokyo 181, Japan

Jan 10, 1984

Dear Friends in Christian Ministry!

Greetings of the New Year in our Lord's name! May 1984 bring new challenges and rich blessings to each of you.

You are probably wondering about the Asian Conference on Pastoral Care and Counseling wich was proposed for 1984 at the Manila Conference in 1982, and again at the San Francisco Congress in 1983. We have been waiting for an official list of people to contact, but failing to obtain that we shall simply write to you as a former participant, and urge you to take the initiative in publicizing this Conference as widely as possible in your country.

We in Japan have followed up on your invitation, and have a voluntary planning committee which has already met several times. We are now prepared to share the following basic information so you can start immediately to plan to attend this conference.

The tentative theme for the program is" Pastoral Care and Counseling in Asian Cultural Contexts". The program will consist mainly of group workshops and some public lectures. One important item will be to discuss the establishing of CPE standards for Asia. If the speaker does not use English, interpretation will be provided.

Travel expense will be the responsibility of each participant. However, we are seeking financial assistance for travel from the Christian Conference of Asia and from sources in Japan. We cannot give definite information about this yet. In the meantime, please try to obtain travel assistance from the national church or ageny to which you belong.

This is just a brief notice so you can start planning your trip to Tokyo. Further information will be sent later. We are hoping for about twenty people from overseas and about eighty from Japan. We know it will be a great conference, not only for study and learning, but for increased mutual understanding among Asian Christians and for warm fellowship.

Sincerely, your colleague

Kenneth J. Dale,

Liaison Secretary

Literature

Adler, Alfred: Religion and individual psychology. New York 1956.

Anderson, Tom: The reflecting team. Dialogues and dialogues about the dialogues. New York 1991

Augsburger, David: Pastoral Counselling Across Cultures. Philadelphia 1986

Augsburger, David: Conflict Mediation Across Cultures. Louisville 1992

Ayete-Nyampong, Samuel: Pastoral Care of the Elderly in Africa: A comparative and cross-cultural study. Accra 2008

Ayete-Nyampong, Samuel: Ageing in Contemporary Ghana. Accra 2008

Baeta, C.G.: Christianitiy and Healing. Orita, 1967

Becher, Werner, Campbell, Alastair, Parker, G. Keith (eds.): The Risks of Freedom. Manila Philippines, May 1993

Becher, Werner (ed.): European Contributions to the International Conferences of Pastoral Care and Counselling from Arnoldshain to Ripon, Arnoldshain 2007

Becher, Werner: International Conferences on Pastoral Care and Counselling, in: *The Journal of Pastoral Care*, Vol. XXXVII, 1983

Becher, Werner (ed.): Clinical Pastoral Education – Klinische Seelsorgeausbildung, Arnoldshain, 1972

Bloomfield, Irene: Helplessness and Omnipotence of the Counsellor. A lecture delivered in Turku 1985, unpublished. Source: Private Documents of Rev. Werner Becher

Bloomfield, Irene: The European Movement for Pastoral Care and Counselling. An Interpretive History, in: Contact, The Interdisciplinary Journal of Pastoral Studies, 1990; p. 16-21

Bloomfield, Irene: Forgiveness and Healing in Human Relationships, unpublished Source: Private Documents of Rev.Werner Becher

Browning, D.S.: Religious Thought and Modern Psychologies: A Critical Conversation in the Theology of Culture; Philadelphia 1987

Boisen, Anton. The exploration of the inner world, New York 1952

Brito, Jorge Cardenas: Case Based Reflections on Contextual Pastoral Care: My Experience in Chile, in: *Stange, Otto (ed.)*: Pastoral Care & Context (lectures from the Congress in Nordwijkerhout), Amsterdam 1992

Browning, D.S.: Citizenship, saintliness and health: relations between religion and the clinical psychological disciplines, in: Contact, The Inter-disciplinary Journal of Pastoral Studies, 1990:2

Burck, J. Russell: German Contributions to Pastoral Care and Counselling; in: The Journal of Pastoral Care, Vol. XXXVII, 1983

Campbell, Alastair, Parker, G. Keith, Becher, Werner (eds.): The Risks of Freedom. Manila Philippines, May 1993

Campbell, Alastair: Helplessness and Omnipotence of the Counsellor. A lecture delivered in Turku 1985. Source: Newsletter of the International Council on Pastoral Care and Counselling, Winter 1986

Campbell, Alastair: Rediscovering Pastoral Care. London 1981

Clebsch, William A. and Jaekle, Charles R.: Pastoral Care in historical perspective. New York, 1975

Clinebell, Howard J.: Basic types of pastoral care and counselling. Resources for the ministry of healing and growth, Nashville 1986

Clinebell, Howard J.: Ecotherapy: healing ourselves, healing the earth. Minneapolis 1996

Coleman, Padraig Berard: Helplessness and Omnipotence of the Counsellor. A lecture delivered in Turku 1985, unpublished Source: Private Documents of Rev. Werner Becher

Contact: The Interdisciplinary Journal of Pastoral Studies, 1982:2, 1984:1, 1988:2 and 1990:2

Cooper, Howard J.: Persecutor and Victim. A lecture delivered in Turku 1985, unpublished
Source: Private Documents of Rev. Werner Becher

Couture, Pamela D., Hunter, Rodney (ed.): Pastoral care and social conflict, Nashville 1995

Couture, Pamela D., Hester, Richard: The future of pastoral care and counseling and the God of the market, in: Hunter, Rodney, Couture, Pamela D.(Ed.): pastoral care and social conflict. Nashville 1995

Cox, John, Ed.: Transcultural Psychiatry, London 1986

Dalton, Albert J.: The Beginning of Clinical Pastoral Care in the Philippines, in: *The Journal of Pastoral Care*, Vol. XXXVII, 1983

Dillen, Annemie, Vandenhoeck, Anne, (eds.): Prophetic Witmess in World Christianities. Rethinking Pastoral Care and Counseling, Münster 2012

Dorn, Roy V.: A Visit to Christian Medical College, Ludhiana, Punjab, India, in: The Journal of Pastoral Care, Vol. XXVII, 1973

Dror, Gilah: Riches, Rivalries and Responsibilities in the Pastoral Coun-

191

selling Setting. A lecture delivered in Ripon, England, 1997. Source: Private Documents of Werner Becher

Dumalagam, Narciso: A brief history of the Asian Conference on Pastoral Care and Counselling. Source: Private Documents of Werner Becher

Elsdörfer, Ulrike, Louw, Daniel, Ito, Takaaki David: Encounter in Pastoral Care and Spiritual Healing, Münster 2012

Elsdörfer, Ulrike: Medizin, Psychologie und Beratung im Islam, Königstein 2007

Elsdörfer, Ulrike: Kirchen in Afrika. Beratung und soziales Engagement, Sulzbach 2011

Erikson, Erik.H.: Childhood and Society, London 1961

Erikson, Erik H.: Identity: Youth and Crisis, New York, 1968

Faber, Heije, Duncan, Denis, Kilbourn, Elizabeth, Kruijne, Teunis: THE NEWSLETTER of the International Committee for Pastoral Care and Counseling, No 2 – Fall 1982

Farris, James: History and Context of the ICPCC, Sao Paolo, 2012

Frankl, Viktor: Man's search for meaning: an introduction for logotherapy. Boston 1959

Friedman, Edwin H.. The Relevance of The Biblical Prophets for Pastoral Counselling

in: *Stange, Otto (ed.)*: Pastoral Care & Context (lectures from the Congress in Nordwijkerhout), Amsterdam 1992

Fromm, Erich: Psychoanalysis and Religion. New York 1951

Foskett, John: Pilgrimage to Poland, in: *The Journal of Pastoral Care*, June 1983, p. 131-135

Gallup, Padmasani J.: "Subham", The Concept of Wholeness in Pastoral Counselling in the Hindu Cultural Context, in: *Stange, Otto (ed.)*: Pastoral Care & Context (lectures from the Congress in Nordwijkerhout), Amsterdam 1992

Graham, Larry Kent: Care of Persons, Care of Worlds: A Psychosystems Approach to Pastoral Care and Counselling, Nashville 1992

Hester, Richard, Couture, Pamela D.: The future of pastoral care and counseling and the God of the market, in: Hunter, Rodney, Couture, Pamela D.(Ed.): pastoral care and social conflict. Nashville 1995

Hiltner, Seward: Theological Dynamics, Nashville 1972

Hiltner, Seward: Preface to pastoral theology. Nashville 1958

Hollenweger, Walter: The Theological Challenge of Indigenous Churches, in: *A. F. Wallsand, W.R. Shenke (eds.)*: Exploring New Religions' Movements, Indiana 1990, p. 163-168

Hulme, William E.: Pastoral Care and Counselling. Using the Unique Resources of the Christian Tradition,, Minneapolis 1981

Hunter, Rodney (ed.), Couture, Pamela D.: Pastoral care and social conflict, Nashville 1995

Hurding, F. Roger: *The Tree of Healing*. London, Ministry Resources Library, 1985.

Hultkrantz, Ake: North American Religions, in: Mircea Eliade: The Encyclopedia of Religion, Vol.10, New York

Igenoza, Andrew Olu: Wholeness in African Experience. Christian perspectives, in: *Lartey, Emmanuel, Nwachuku, Daisy, Kasonga wa Kasonga (eds.)* : The Church and Healing: Echoes from Africa, in. African Pastoral Studies,Vol. 2, Frankfurt/Main 1991, p. 125/126

Ito, Takaaki David, Elsdörfer, Ulrike, Louw, Daniel: Encounter in Pastoral Care and Spiritual Healing, Münster 2012

Kakar, Sudhir, (ed.): Identity and Adulthood, Delhi 1979

Kakar, Sudhir: The Inner World. A Psychoanalytic Study of Childhood and Society in India, Delhi 1978

Kalu,Wilhelmina: Gospel and Pastoral Counselling in Africa, in: *Stange, Otto (ed.)*: Pastoral Care & Context (lectures from the Congress in Nordwijkerhout), Amsterdam 1992

Kasonga wa Kasonga: African christian palaver: A contemporary way of healing communal conflicts and crises, in: *Lartey, Emmanuel, Nwachuku, Daisy, Kasonga wa Kasonga (eds.)*: The Church and Healing: Echoes from Africa, in. African Pastoral Studies, Vol. 2, Frankfurt/Main 1991, P. 49-65

Keidel, Keith W.: Cross-Cultural Clinical Pastoral Training in Singapore, in: The Journal of Pastoral Care, Vol. XXVII, 1973

Lartey, Emmanuel, Nwachuku, Daisy, Kasonga wa Kasonga (eds.): The Church and Healing: Echoes from Africa, in. African Pastoral Studies, Vol. 2, Frankfurt/Main 1991, Appendix: Background of the African Association for Pastoral Studies and Counselling and information on the series, p. 154

Lartey, Emmanuel Y.: In Living Colour, Philadelphia 2003

Lartey, Immanuel Y.: Globalization, Internalization and Indigenization of Pastoral Care and Counselling, in: Pastoral Care and Counselling: Redefining the Pradigms, 2004

Literature

Lartey, Emmanuel Y.: Pastoral Theology in an Intercultural World; Suffolk, UK and USA 2006

Lartey, Emmanuel Y.: Two healing communities in Africa, in: *Lartey, Emmanuel, Nwachuku, Daisy, Kasonga wa Kasonga (eds.)*: The Church and Healing: Echoes from Africa, in: African Pastoral Studies, Vol. 2, Frankfurt/Main 1991, p. 35-48

Lartey, Emmanuel Y.: Some Contextual Implications for Pastoral Counselling in Ghana, in: *Masamba ma Mpolo, Jean, Nwachuku, Daisy (eds.)*: Pastoral Care and Counselling in Africa Today, in: African Pastoral Studies, Vol. 1, Frankfurt/Main 1991, p. 34-44

Louw, Daniel, Ito, Takaaki David, Elsdörfer, Ulrike: Encounter in Pastoral Care and Spiritual Healing, Münster 2012

Louw, Daniel J.: Meaning in Suffering: A theological reflection on the cross and the resurrection for pastoral care and counselling, Frankfurt 2000

Louw, Daniel J.: Curae Vitae. Illness and the healing of life, Wellington 2005

Lutahoire, Sebastian K.: The Risks of Freedom – a response, in*: Becher, Werner, Campbell, Alastair, Parker, G. Keith (eds.): The Risks of Freedom. Manila Philippines, May 1993, p. 39-41*

Marteau, Louis: A short history of Pastoral Care and Counseling in Great Britain and its present challenge, in: The Journal of Pastoral Care, Vol. XXVII, 1973

Manitowabi, Edna: Native Stories for Transition in a Strange Land. Contribution to the 5th International Congress on Pastoral Care and Counselling, in: Babylon and Jerusalem. Stories for Transition in a Strange Land, ed. by James Reed, Toronto, Canada

Masamba ma Mpolo, Jean, Nwachuku, Daisy (eds.): Pastoral Care and Counselling in Africa Today, in: African Pastoral Studies, Vol. 1, Frankfurt/Main 1991

Masamba ma Mpolo, Jean: Spirituality and Counselling for healing and liberation: The context and praxis of African pastoral activity and psychotherapy, in: *Lartey, Emmanuel, Nwachuku, Daisy, Kasonga wa Kasonga (eds.)*: The Church and Healing: Echoes from Africa, in: African Pastoral Studies, Vol. 2, Frankfurt/Main 1991, p. 11-35

Masamba ma Mpolo, Jean: A Brief Review of Psychiatric Research in Africa: Some implications to Pastoral Counselling, in: *Masamba ma Mpolo, Jean, Nwachuku, Daisy (eds.)*: Pastoral Care and Counselling in Africa Today, in: African Pastoral Studies, Vol. 1, Frankfurt/Main 1991, p. 9-33

Masamba ma Mpolo, Jean: Freedom and culture: in: *Becher, Werner, Campbell,*

Alastair, Parker, G. Keith (eds.): The Risks of Freedom. Manila Philippines, May 1993, p. 109-125

Mbiti, John S.: Bible and Theology in African Christianity, Nairobi 1986

Mbiti, John S.: New Testament Eschatology in an African Background, Oxford 1971

McNeill, John T.: A history of the cure of souls, New York, 1951

Mitchell, Kenneth: CPE Experiences in the Netherlands, in: *The Journal of Pastoral Care*, Vol. XXVII, 1973

Moltmann, Jürgen: The Risks of Freedom, in: Becher, Werner, Campbell, Alastair, Parker, G. Keith (eds.): The Risks of Freedom. Manila Philippines, May 1993, p. 9-41

Niebuhr, H.R. and Williams, Daniel (eds.): The ministry in historical perpective. New York 1975

Ostermann, Horst: The history of the CPE – movement in the Philippines, 2001

Otto, Rudolf: The Idea of the Holy. London, Oxford Press, 1923.

Parker, Keith: Rüschlikon 1975, Formation for Ministry: Memories, Dreams and Reflections, in: the a.p.p.c. Journal, Association for Pastoral Care and Counselling, 1985

Parker, G. Keith, Becher, Werner, Campbell, Alastair V.(eds.): The Risks of Freedom. Manila Philippines, May 1993

Patton, John: Pastoral Care in Context, Louisville 1993

Patton, John: Pastoral Care. An Essential Guide, Nashville 2005

Patton, John: The International Pastoral Care and Counseling Movement. What Is It?, in: *The Journal of Pastoral Care*, June 1983, p. 81-85

Pedersen, Paul: Intercultural criteria for mental health training, in: *Pedersen, Paul (ed.)* Handbook of cross-cultural counseling and therapy, London 1987

Perls, Frederic: The Gestalt Approach and Eye Witness to Therapy, Palo Alto 1976

Pobee, John S.: Toward an African Theology, Nashville 1979

Pobee, John S.: African Spirituality, in: *Gordon Wakefield (ed.)*: A Dictionary of Christian Spirituality, London 1983

Pobee, John S.: Religion and politics in Ghana, Accra 1991

Pobee, John S.: Kwame Nkrumah and the Church in Ghana 1949-1966, Accra 1988

Reed, James: Babylon and Jerusalem. Stories for Transition in a Strange Land (lectures from the Congress in Toronto), 1995, internal document

Riedel-Pfäfflin, Ursula, Smith, Archie: Siblings by choice: Race, Gender, and Violence, St. Louis 2004

Sahin, Fuad: Islam Stories for Transition in a Strange Land. Contribution to the 5th International Congress on Pastoral Care and Counselling, in: Babylon and Jerusalem. Stories for Transition in a Strange Land, ed. by James Reed, Toronto, Canada

Sathler-Rosa, Ronaldo: Pastoral action in post-modern time: A brazilian perspective, in: Intercultural Pastoral Care and Counseling, No. 1, 1996

Schipani, Daniel S., Dawn Buchert, Leah (eds). Interfaith Spiritual Care: Understandings and Practices. Ontario, Canada 2009.

Schneider-Harpprecht: Interkulturelle Seelsorge, Göttingen 2001

Smith, Archie, Riedel-Pfäfflin, Ursula: Siblings by choice: Race, Gender, and Violence, St. Louis 2004

Shorter, Alyward: African Christian Theology, London 1975

Sotheren, Douglas I.: Clinical Pastoral Counseling: An Australian Model, in: The Journal of Pastoral Care, Vol. XXXVII, 1983

Stange, Otto (ed.): Pastoral Care & Context (lectures from the Congress in Nordwijkerhout), Amsterdam 1992

Sugunasiri, Suwanda H.J.: Buddhist Stories for Transition in a Strange Land. Contribution to the 5th International Congress on Pastoral Care and Counselling, in: Babylon and Jerusalem. Stories for Transition in a Strange Land, ed. by James Reed, Toronto, Canada

Swan, Susan: The transformative Power of Story. Contribution to the 5th International Congress on Pastoral Care and Counselling, in: Babylon and Jerusalem. Stories for Transition in Strange Land, ed. by James Reed, Toronto, Canada

ten Dulk; Marten: Contextuality: A Theological Paradigm,in: *Stange, Otto (ed.)*: Pastoral Care & Context (lectures from the Congress in Nordwijkerhout), Amsterdam 1992

Tillich, Paul: Dynamics of Faith. New York 1953

Tillich, Paul: The Courage to Be, New Haven 1952

The Journal of Pastoral Care: June 1973, 2 and 1983, 2

The Journal for African History: Vol. 48, Cambridge, USA, Nov. 2007

Vandenhoeck, Anne, Dillen, Annemie (Eds.): Prophetic Witmess in World Christianities. Rethinking Pastoral Care and Counseling, Münster 2012

van Deusen Hunsinger, Deborah: Theology & Pastoral Counseling. A New Interdisciplinary Approach. Michigan 1995

Voytovich, Steven: A Multicultural Typology, in: *Weiss, Helmut, Temme,*

Literature

Klaus (ed.): Treasure in Earthen Vessels. Intercultural Perspectives on Pastoral Care Facing Fragility and Destruction, Münster 2009

Watzlawick, Paul et.al.: Pragmatics of Human Communication, New York 1967

Wainwright, Elaine M.: Women Healing/Healing Women, London 2006

Weiss, Helmut, Temme, Klaus (eds.): Treasure in Earthen Vessels. Intercultural Perspectives on Pastoral Care Facing Fragility and Destruction, Münster 2009

Wilkinson, John: The Bible and Healing. A Medical and Theological Commentary, Grand Rapids, 1998

Winnicott, D.W.: Playing and Reality. New York, Penguin 1974

Pastoral Care and Spiritual Healing
edited by Daniël Johannes Louw (Stellenbosch) Ulrike Elsdörfer (Frankfurt) and
Stéphan van der Watt (Tokushima)

Daniël Louw; Takaaki David Ito; Ulrike Elsdörfer (Eds.)
Encounter in Pastoral Care and Spiritual Healing
Towards an integrative and intercultural approach
The International Council on Pastoral Care and Counselling (ICPCC) met in August 2011 in Rotorua / New Zealand for its 9th International Congress.
Various approaches to the field arose from actual challenges as the earthquake in Japan or social changes and mainly deprivations all over the world. Spiritual Care and Counselling gives guidelines to cope with the situations.
Regarding indigenous traditions from Maori culture or projects on interreligious encounter: both provoke a rethinking of traditional spirituality. The proceedings present the state of discussion within this globalized network.

LIT Verlag Berlin – Münster – Wien – Zürich – London
Auslieferung Deutschland / Österreich / Schweiz: siehe Impressumsseite